MY LIFE IN A JAR

THE BOOK OF

BY **SMO** AND **JAKE BROWN**

Published by: SMO-Motion Publishing/Baker & Taylor

Text Design by: Darlene Swanson/van-garde.com

Cover Design by: John Lee Smith and Bryn Person

Editor: SB Lewis

A CIP record for this book is available from the Library of Congress Cataloging-in-Publication Data

ISBN: 9780692139998

Distributed by: BAKER & TAYLOR
30 Amberwood Pkwy, Ashland, OH 44805

Printed and bound in Location by McNaughton-Gunn
www.mcnaughton-gunn.com

Dedication & Thanks

This book is dedicated to my parents, Carl "Killer" Smith and Mary Jane Smith. Y'all made one hell of a world for this ole boy. THANK YOU for everything! To my three beautiful daughters Ameria, Ansley, and Lanica — I love and cherish each of you. To my closest circle of true friends, THANK YOU! I appreciate your patience and support for many years, and I look forward to our future. To my KINFOKE, what can I say? You've made this journey so incredible in countless ways. Everything we have experienced together; words will never do justice! YOU are the gas in the SMOmotion Locomotion that will never stop pushin' down this rebel road!

Thank you!

KINFOKE4LIFE

"If you can't say something nice about someone, don't say nothing at all!

~ Momma Smo

This book was handcrafted for the non-reader as well as the avid page-turner. When the font is larger throughout the book, it's me speaking. Whenever it's smaller, it's my Kinfoke.

Hope you enjoy,

~ SMO

Contents

The Guest List

1. John Rich – Big & Rich/Friend

2. Chris Smith – Brother

3. Travis Fults – Childhood Friend

4. Mary Jane Smith – aka Momma Smo

5. Andy Milhauser – High School Friend

6. Tommy Donegan – Family Friend

7. Tyrone Watts – Brother from Another Mother

8. "Ray 'Orig the DJ' Riddle – DJ/Producer/Friend

9. JJ – Longtime Friend

10. Haystak – Mentor/Southern Rap Legend

11. Jon Conner – Producer/Videographer

12. Charlie Bonnet III – Guitar player 2010 – 2012

13. Jeff McCool – aka Brahma Bull

14. Relapse – Co-Writer/Rapper/Friend

15. Dan Nelson – Manager (2012 – 2017)

16. Frank Wing – Booking Agent (2011 – 2018)

17. Haden Carpenter – Hypeman (2014 – 2016)

18. Bob Gillam – A&E TV Show Producer

19. Rhett Akins – Nashville Songwriter

20. Ameria Smith – Daughter

21. Lanica Smith – Daughter

22. Mike Lowrey – Security/Bus Driver

23. Steve and Ladybug – Family Friends

24. Kuntry – Kinfoke Brother

25. Matt Julian – Kinfoke Brother

26. Jason Mater – Producer (2015 – 2018)

27. Bird Brooks – The Moonshine Bandits

28. Demun Jones – Hick Hop Artist

29. Clay Sharpe – The LACs

30. Shannon Houchins – Average Joes Entertainment

31. David 'D-Ray' Ray – Producer/Friend

Foreword: John Rich

I was on my tour bus with Cowboy Troy looking at unsigned artists and new music on YouTube. We always plug the laptop into the stereo to hear the music really loud. That night, we ran across this guy Big Smo. I remember thinking, "Okay, this guy is interesting," because here's this big, white guy rapping, and as Cowboy Troy would say, "That boy goes hard." Then we got to the part of the video for *Kickin' It in Tennessee* where he chops the chicken's head off! When I saw that, I told Troy, "Back that up, let me see that again! Did he really just do that?? This boy ain't playing around!"

The first thing that got me about him was his tone. He could sing the alphabet in that voice and you'd probably go buy it! He's convincing when he delivers his flow. It's all part of connecting to the listener. That piqued my interest in him even more, so I started looking up more of his music. I reached out to say, "Hey, I'm a fan of your music, keep it going." He hit me back and I wound up inviting him over to my house. We've had some long talks over the years about music. He's opened for Big & Rich and I was on his TV show. It's a great back and forth relationship. As I got to know him, I felt the cool thing about Smo is he genuinely is that person. He's got that edge to him, but he's also a family guy. He's patriotic; he cares about the country and our military, and he does a lot of things for a lot of people behind the scenes. That's something I have a great deal of respect for.

To me, he rides a unique line because country rap is not a major genre. Even Cowboy Troy will tell you that rap about country stuff is not mainstream. Even though, in my opinion, it should be. When you mix it all up and do it well like Smo does, there's a huge market for that. He really is a pioneer in a genre that has not seen its full potential. I feel like his contributions to this unique sound make him an important figure in that world. Smo's artistic twist turned on a lot of ears to the country rap genre for the first time.

Artists that are unafraid like Smo are rare. He creates art that leaves his mark. He's nothing like anyone I know. It takes a lot of courage to be who you truly are. That a real artist's spirit! After he got signed on a major label as the first artist in the Country Rap genre, I saw his character and ability to prove to people that what he's doing is legit, because it is. I can tell you there's traditionally not a lot of room for such a unique individual, but Smo was able to go in there and carve a place out for himself. The same thing happened with his TV show. There were millions of people a week tuning in to watch this guy! He believes in his art and loves what he does and the Kinfoke he does it for. Anytime I can do anything for Smo I will because he's the Real McCoy.

SHOWTIME!

Five more minutes to go. I take the in-ears set and microphone from my tour manager. The steam from my hot tea soothes my throat. It's a stark contrast from the moonshine and Red Stag I relied on to get ready for so many shows before this one. Not anymore. Throat Coat tea with lots of honey is key. I adjust my outfit and hit the head one last time. The green room is dingy and dimly lit. I pull a Sharpie out of my pocket and tag the usual "Smo was here" among the other famous and unknown names. I can hear the crowd before I even see them. The pounding of the kick-drum vibrates my chest and the faces in the front row illuminate under the stage lights before I even make the turn. I say a quick prayer and hop up on the stage.

It's showtime.

Part I:
In The Beginning

Chapter 1:
The Smackeroo Madman

My daddy taught me that if you earn your way
It will mean more to ya when you spend it some day
Keep savin' up ya change, never throw it away
Fill ya jar to the top and put it somewhere safe.

~ **My Life in a Jar**

From the time I can first remember, my dad called me John Boy. He used to say, "John Boy, Smackeroo Madman, eating out of the garbage can!" I never knew why, but he called me that all the time. I loved my dad. He's always been my hero.

Momma Smo: My husband's nickname – which everybody always called him – was *Killer*. My mother and Aunt Margaret were sisters, and my Aunt Margaret married Carl's Uncle Cecil. His grandparents raised him and his two siblings after their mother died when they were very young. Aunt Margaret and Uncle Cecil were at this gathering and Carl was with them because he happened to be on leave. I got stood up for a date, so Carl offered to drive me home. After that, Carl started showing up every day! We used to go to the Supper Club on Saturday nights to dance with

Aunt Margaret and Uncle Cecil. Carl and his brother Don used to go too. We dated the whole time he was home on leave. He took me to football games, but I didn't know anything about football, so I had to pretend I knew all about it.

When we got married, I found myself on my first airplane ever to Florida. We got married in Jacksonville, and Carl took me to this really nice restaurant. Our table had this curtain around it and musicians were playing instruments. They brought out this HUGE pizza! I'd never had pizza before in my life! I took one bite of it and couldn't eat anymore. Carl on the other hand ate the whole thing! I thought he would die that night!

I was born in San Diego, California at Balboa Hospital. My dad, Chief Carl Avery Smith, was stationed at Imperial Beach. He was a career Navy man and had already served 25 years by the time I was born. I am the unexpected byproduct of a last-minute weekend trip to Vegas. My mom didn't even believe it when she found out she was pregnant because she was almost 40 and my dad was 42.

> **Momma Smo:** It was a shock to say the least when Carl found out I was pregnant with John. At the time, I was an office manager on the Naval Base. I thought I had the flu or was having a nervous breakdown because I just felt awful. I had no earthly idea I was expecting. It had been twenty years since I had last been pregnant with John's older half-sister! When I went to the infirmary on the base, they had me take a pregnancy test right there on the spot. I remember a young girl was sitting in the chair beside me, here I am 37, and they came out and told her she wasn't pregnant. They looked at me and said, "But *you are*!" I looked over at the young girl and said, "The military

screwed up again! You must be pregnant because I'm not! I'm a grandmother!"

Once it sunk in that I was, in fact, pregnant, I went back to the office and called my husband who was out at sea at the time. When I finally got him on the line, I asked him, "Are you sitting down?" He said, "No, why?" I said "Well, I think you better grab you a chair because you're going to be a father." There were a couple seconds of silence, then he dropped the phone!

Sometimes Carl would pick up celebrities from the airport when they flew in for appearances. He even picked up Bob Hope once. He loved to play golf and would take them along with him. A lot of times he would play by himself, so naturally he was on the golf course and unreachable when I went into labor. My girlfriend had to take me to the hospital, and by the time Carl got there, it was late that night. I was in hard labor with John Lee for 48 hours! He was 8 pounds, 8 ounces with a BIG head. When he was coming out, his head got squished during a pause in contractions. Carl joked with everybody that he was going to throw him into a dart board! My husband was quite a joker.

John was into everything! He was in his high chair in the kitchen once. I looked away and when I turned back around, he had those little feet climbing up the refrigerator. Another time I found him in a hallway where I kept all my nice china in a cabinet. He had them all pulled out and was up in the shelf of the cabinet! I went into the bathroom and he'd gotten up on the commode and climbed into the sink – that's the kind of child he was.

When we were stationed in San Diego, we lived on a busy corner. Of course, because my husband was away at sea a lot, I had to do the yard work while taking care of John. I tried everything. I took the playpen out there but that didn't work because he'd climb out. I thought about tying him to a tree but thought I'd get accused of child abuse. I would have to carry him on my hip while I pushed an electric lawnmower and mowed the yard.

After his 26th year in the Navy, my dad retired and we moved back to Bedford County, Tennessee, where both my parents' families had grown up. My dad had some land and wanted to raise me there. Proudly, it's still where I live today with my family.

Carl A Smith Retirement

Good Ole Carl #GOUSA

Momma Smo: It made sense to move back to Tennessee to raise John. Carl missed his younger years, so when he retired, he wanted us to move back. California was a fast-paced life, and we lived close to the border. It was pretty dangerous. We thought it was best to get out of there. I had a really good job and he'd just been promoted to Chief, but in 1980, we decided to pack up the camper on the back of Carl's blue Chevy pickup. It had a queen-sized bed over the cab and a little dining table that turned into John's bed. We stopped at KOA sites along the way across the country. At one of the campsites, Carl took John swimming for the first time! We made it to Tennessee to our ten-acre farm. Carl had to get all the equipment to keep up with the place and it seems like he rode the tractor nonstop!

Margaret Cecelia Smith Crow
September 11, 1956-October 17, 1980

Chapter 2:

Farm Life

I'm a full-time father and a stand-up brother
Always been a problem
You can ask my mother
Cause I came up on Hank and Cash
Beastie Boys came after that
DMC, NWA
But Skynyrd always takes me back
~ Country Outlaw

My parents were happy to settle back home, but tragedy struck when my sister was killed in a motorcycle accident. I was 4 years old at the time, and only remember her in flashes. My sister had a son and he came to live with us. He was 3 years older than me, and we were instantly best friends! I was so excited to have a big brother, even though we chuckle about it today because technically, my older brother is actually my nephew. We were raised together, and from the time I can remember, he was always in my life.

> **Momma Smo:** Carl adopted my daughter Sissy, who I had before we ever got married, and raised her up like she was his. He always treated Sissy like he treated John. He and

my grandson Christopher were raised up as brothers after my daughter was killed at 24 in a motorcycle accident and we took my grandson in. John never really got to know his sister, but he and Chris always called each other brothers even though John is really his uncle. The farm was great for them to grow up together.

Chris Smith, Smo's Older Brother: Papa was a great man and he cared a lot about me and John. He was very active in both our lives, trying to keep us involved in community things growing up, whether it was sports or scouts.

The Pinewood Derby was a big deal in the Scouts for the three of us. It was always a competition between me and John, but with Papa helping both of us. We each had our own way we wanted to design our cars, and we actually had a pinewood derby track at home! I don't know how he got it, but he had it set up out in the garage. I remember thinking, "Wow, we got a Pinewood Derby track at home!" Every year, we would race our past model cars and our new ones, and I think it gave us an edge. As an extra leg up on top of that, he worked at an Air Force base and was always interested in the latest technology for lubrication. He would have us use graphite on the wheels just so we could get less friction! He was at that level of involvement, but he'd share with everybody and anybody in our troop. He would always hook them up.

Travis Fults, Smo's First Best Friend: John and Carl were inseparable. Carl was our Cub Scouts leader and that's where our friendship started. Carl was awesome. He was big on Pinewood Derby cars! John Lee always had a better car than I did. I remember one time thinking his looked like a Corvette and mine looked like a Pinto.

We were always into doing something outside, we used to go on camping trips to Cumberland Caverns. It was a big deal to me because it's such a cool place. They even have a big chandelier hanging inside of the cave! I can probably say Carl's one of the greatest people I've known in my life.

Me & Travis Fults fishing in the Scouts

In Tennessee, I grew up on a 12-acre farm with cows and a barn and a creek by the woods. I LOVED cows!

I remember as a young kid, we had a calf born prematurely. The veterinarian told us, "You're going to have to bottle-feed this calf." I took on that responsibility and it became a pet. My routine was to get home and go out in the field to find my calf. I would get on my hands and knees and butt heads with it! That could have been part of my problem later in life-I butted heads with too many cows as a kid. One morning, I was catching the bus when I saw a weird truck and trailer loading my calf. That was when I realized pets come and go. I loved feeding the cows. Chris and I were both a lot less enthusiastic about digging fence posts and chopping thistles.

Chris: The big thing we used to do was ride a go-cart all around the field. It was a single-ride, 3 horse power go-cart that Uncle Cecil gave us. It was like a rocket. We had to dodge the cow patties, because if we hit that with a tire, it would make it rain manure. We had all kinds of fun!

Breakfast was a staple in our family and may be why I wound up having heart surgery at 39 (spoiler alert). It was a platter of biscuits, bacon, sausage, country ham, fried and scrambled eggs, and hash browns – the whole table was like a buffet. I would pile it all together and then pour GRAVY over the whole plate. I would take country ham and bust it down on top of the gravy. If I was lucky enough to get my hands on a little bit of pancake syrup, I would put that on top of all of it. The funny thing is, the rest of my family didn't eat like this, so I was entertainment for them. They would watch in amazement as I created this masterpiece of flavor, and by the time they were done eating, I was just starting. This was two or three times a week, so if you want to have heart surgery, boys and girls, that's a good way to start!

Travis: When we were kids, he blended everything. He didn't start with music, he started with food and drinks. He would take 3 or 4 different flavors of Kool-Aid and mix them together or take food and blend it. I always joke it's appropriate that he's a rapper because he's like a Ninja Blender. He's done that since we were little.

Mom was always cooking. In fact, there wasn't a time I can recall growing up when she wasn't cooking something, and we always had the best food. The only weekly meal I wasn't that crazy about was Sunday supper with my grandmother. She was as mean as SNAKE SPIT. I'm serious, I don't know if I've ever met another woman as mean as my grandmother.

My dad also owned two sides of Temple Fort Road. We named it Green Acres and explored it every weekend. He prided himself on how beautiful his property was. It was a playground for us to grow up in. We spent a lot of time on Sugar Creek wading, fishing, and shooting snakes. As I got older, my dad took us down to the other end of Green Acres. We were clearing off brush when we discovered this old abandoned smokehouse on our land. It later became the "Smotel". It was always my favorite thing to get to drive the truck to take the trash to the dump. I started driving back when we were clearing the land and me and Chris always fought over who got to drive when we were little.

Those were the same woods where we went every year to cut down our Christmas Tree! One Christmas, I asked for a red SHS-10 Yamaha Synthesizer Key-Tar, which was a combination keyboard and guitar. I remember wanting it so bad because I was fascinated with music. My mom and dad loved Christmas. My mom hung stockings she'd made herself that had our names sewn on them.

Even in the early years, we knew who our Santa list was really going to, so instead of milk and cookies, we left out a PBR and bag of pretzels. My parents hid our presents under a shifty board in the attic. Sure enough, curiosity always got the best of me and I kept sneaking up there looking for one box in particular. I snuck up there and found the shape of a Key-tar wrapped in Santa paper. I thought, "Hell yeah! It's on like Donkey Kong!" (I was like 8).

Around the house, I listened to the Oldies with my dad. There was something about the sound of the trumpet. I really liked it. My parents bought me one and I tried out for the band in 7th grade. After the trumpet, I switched to drum line to be with my buddies. The band director stuck me with the bass drum because I was big enough to carry it.

Besides music, I LOVED movies. The first VHS tapes my dad brought home from my aunt Marie's video store were *The Neverending Story* and *Pieces*. My parents let us pop in the second movie instead of making us go to bed. Contrary to *The Neverending Story*, *Pieces* was about a serial killer that cuts bodies up and stitches them back together! That was it for me! My life-long love and fascination with horror began! My Uncle Tommy—who looked and strangely enough, sang like Kenny Rogers – lived in town and had H.B.O.

He recorded Friday the 13th every time it would come on. He recorded them all – *Parts 1 - 5* (at the time)– and labeled them on top of each tape. It was amazing.

I liked special effects artist Tom Savini the best. From the machete in the side of the head to the blood that flew off the blade when it sliced down into the skull, he did it all! H.B.O. had specials with the Effects Artist at the end of the movies. It was always Tom Savini. I was so intrigued that this guy's job was to make GORE. As a kid if you asked me what I wanted to be when I grew up, I said a special effects artist! I thought being able to create a knife going through somebody's head was art. I wanted to be the dude that showed up on the movie set with buckets of fake blood and limbs ready to start chopping heads off. I didn't wait until I was an adult to start working toward that goal either. I imitated my favorite horror movie special effects from Freddy Kruger to Michael Myers. Once I got into the cult classics, I really dug in deep. I even subscribed to Fangoria Magazine.

My room looked like a Halloween store because I had masks, movie posters, and Christmas lights strung up all over. My mom made this doll that was a life-sized baby. It was so weird, and I decided it was the perfect target for my next Frankenstein experiment. I Chucky-dolled the shit out of this poor baby doll. I sliced that thing apart! I made an incision on the doll, then glued it back. I went in with fake blood and some Sharpie on the outside like a stitch and then I dirtied it up around the wound. It was really no different than painting. When I was finished, I was so proud of my creation that I hung it from a rope from the ceiling fan. It even had a Freddy Kruger glove and the Jason Voorhees mask! To add to the decor, Aunt Marie gave me the cardboard stand-ups from the new horror movies from her video store. I had them all: *Nightmare on Elm Street, Halloween, Hell Raiser, Evil Dead, Creepshow*. My room got so full of these cardboard stand-ups that it looked like a House of Horrors.

Here's a funny story: I was home alone after my parents had put the house up for sale when these ladies stopped by and asked if they could look inside. We started out downstairs then they asked if they could see upstairs. I said, "Sure, come on up!" They followed me through the beaded curtains that led into my room. You'd have thought they walked into the Texas Chainsaw Massacre house! It was classic. Their eyes got wider and wider. Then they saw the doll hanging from the ceiling fan with a knife sticking out of it! They FREAKED out and ran out of the house. Then, they asked if they could PRAY with me because my room was an "abomination." I said, "HELL NO!" Needless to say, they didn't buy our house.

Chris was a big influence on me. We were in Scouts, played sports, and did everything together. Some of my favorite memories are the summers we spent at Camp Boxwell. I learned so much from him. One time at Camp Boxwell, a kid was drowning. Chris wrapped a rope around his waist, jumped in the river, and saved him! He was a hero! I was so proud. He always had my back no matter what. I tagged along with his friends and they always bumped the coolest music. He got me into Grandmaster Flash, Run DMC, and the Beastie Boys. I LOVED the Fat Boys! I thought I was one of them! We also liked a lot of rock so when Def Leppard came out with *Pour Some Sugar on Me*, I used to perform like a rock star. My "ah ha!" moment happened when Vanilla Ice first hit with *Ice Ice Baby*.

I had an epiphany, "Wow! A white boy can do this?!" I LOVED Vanilla Ice. He helped light that hope in me way back in the day. I caught the bug for rhyming, and as hip hop grew, I grew up right along with it. Where we lived there wasn't much hip-hop influence. We got this VHS tape called *Breakin'* and we tried to do our own Brooklyn street dance B-Boy DJ stuff right there on the farm. We had the *Breakin'* movie soundtrack and the poster with step-by-step break-dancing moves on it. I even did a performance at a dance at my grade school. My buddy and I stuffed pillows under our shirts and came out on stage to perform Fat Boys *Wipe Out*. I knew at 10 years old, "This is who I am!"

> **Momma Smo:** The boys would take my husband's VCR camera and lip-sync the Fat Boys, D.J. Jazzy Jeff, and the Fresh Prince *Parents Just Don't Understand*. They'd record

themselves and pretend they were doing the singing. They did pretty good with all the words!

Travis: John would always play Run DMC and the Beastie Boys back when we were hanging out at his house. I was into Hank Jr., so I kind of got him listening to Hank. He became a BIG Hank Jr. fan and even had a red '57 Chevy model car he decorated with Hank Jr. all over it. He got me listening to Run D.M.C., and that's kind of funny now!

As a young kid, we got tapes in the mail from RCA. My dad never sang, but he loved music. I remember listening to Jerry Reed's *The Bird* in his truck when 8-tracks were still around. He was into old country like Conway Twitty, Willie Nelson, Johnny Cash, and Hank Williams. He was old school. I listened to those 8-tracks with him, especially the songs that told a story like Old Western Country. He was such a funny guy.

Chris and I became master pranksters as we got older! Out in the country with nothing to do, we had to invent our own fun. Our favorite prank was stealing tomatoes out of mom's garden and stringing them across the highway from one telephone pole to the other. We would hide in the barn loft and watch until SPLAT! Tomato guts everywhere! Then, brakes screeching and yelling, "Damn kids!"

Chris: We thought we were gangster pranksters, so we called it "*Ganking*" instead of "*Pranking*."

Another signature gankin' move was The Moss Toss. Basically we slung moss onto windshields with a broom handle. Looking back, I can see this was really dangerous, but, thankfully, no one got hurt. Our family was really big on fireworks. My Uncle Albert owned a fireworks stand so we got the hook up on whatever we wanted. My dad got us these big rockets, not like bottle rockets, but like the kind that are perfect for making a homemade bazooka. With a piece of PVC pipe and a plastic cup on the end, all Chris had to do was drop the lit rocket into the end and we had our very own RPG. I would aim it and it would whistle out of the end like a missile.

One night that rocket shot out and got stuck in the grill of a tractor trailer that was barreling down the road. I couldn't have hit that truck if I had tried! The brakes locked up and a huge man jumped out and came hauling ass up the driveway. "You could have killed me! Where's your parents?" Luckily, it was a Thursday night pot luck at the VFW.

Our neighbor had a beautiful Corvette that was his pride and joy. We were launching smoke bombs with slingshots across the field and I aimed for the open garage door. I thought, "There's no way I'm going to hit this!" Next thing I know, green smoke came rolling out from under the Corvette. To this day, I don't know how I didn't get caught for that.

As you can probably assume, Chris and I were a bit of pyromaniacs as kids. Chris made a Molotov cocktail with a baby jar, a greasy shop rag, and some engine starter fluid. When it started burning and stinking, we were scared we would blow up the garage, or worse, get caught by mom. Chris kicked the burning baby jar out the back door of the garage while our friends stood guard. Next thing we know, the entire two-acre field by our house was a raging inferno!

> **Momma Smo:** When I first walked in, I knew something was going on. They told me everything was fine, but behind them through the garage windows, I could see all this smoke rising! I kicked open the back door and sure enough, the field behind our house was on fire! I about killed 'em! They could have burned the garage and the neighbor's house down if I hadn't caught them when I did. You BETTER believe they got their butts WHOOPED that night!

When it came to get a good whoopin', dad's preference was his belt. He had this way of yanking it out of the loops to where it slung around like a snake. It made that pop sound a dad's worn leather belt makes right before you get it. Don't get me wrong, we always deserved it when dad got that belt out. He loved his belt. Mom preferred switches off the peach tree. She lined up right next to dad to wait her turn! As I got older and bigger, the switches weren't effective, so mom beat me with a breadboard. Not only did it break the board, but it came close to breaking her wrist!

> **Momma Smo:** He had a butt of concrete! You've heard that expression, "This is gonna hurt me more than it will hurt you," well *it did*. It sent me to the *chiropractor*.

> **Andy:** I first met Smo back in 1990 when I gave him and his neighbor a ride home from school. He had a box-top haircut with "Ice Ice Baby" shaved into the back of his

head. I knew from that moment we'd be good friends. He got in the car to go to a concert once and his mom hung her head out the back door. "John Lee, did you forget your Ganking clothes?" He said, "No mom, I got 'em!" I remember thinking, "What on earth is gankin'?

My mom had no idea what *Ganking* meant, she just heard us say it all the time. We had this buddy Jason that lived on top of the hill above Southside Elementary School. We hit up an old lady's garden and headed down to the playground on the main highway running through town. I showed them how to string up vegetables across the road. Now at 3 in the morning, there wasn't a lot of traffic except for the POLICE, of course. A patrol car came flying down the road when SPLAT! Instantly, BLUE LIGHTS! We hid all over the playground while they walked around with searchlights. Somehow, they never found a single one of us!

I was so excited getting away with all our tricks that I took the money I had saved up and went to a guy that did airbrush out of a trailer parked in town. He made us t-shirts with flying tomatoes and exploded melons all over it. They said, "Southside Ganking Posse". Not long after that, I graduated from fruit and veggie bombs.

At that age, I was a huge MacGyver fan. In one particular episode, he dumped the powder out of shotgun shells and a used light bulb to make a grenade. I just so happened to have shotgun shells and a light bulb. Needless to say, I felt inspired.

> **Andy:** I fell in love with the idea, so we got this older dude to buy us a keg of black gun powder. We went back to my house and stole my parents' little Jack Daniel's bottles. We packed them full of gun powder and wrapped them in socks and duct-tape. We got done making them and were like, "What are we going to do with all these bombs?"

First, we set one off and blew a crater in their gravel driveway! Then we had the genius idea to put one in a mailbox.

> **Andy:** The first one that we put a bomb in probably blew up 100 feet from the house. It twisted inside out and looked like Terminator 2! We loved that so much that we decided to keep going until we ran out of bombs.

We targeted the fancy mailboxes with the brick around them. Andy drove while I hung out the passenger window sticking a bomb in each of the boxes. I lit the fuse and Andy drove far enough away where we could still watch the BOOM! A fireball and mushroom cloud exploded out of the hole where the box had been. We blew up over 17 mailboxes that night. We still had some powder left, so we decided to upgrade our bomb design from airplane bottles to a mason jar. Highway 231 was just two lanes back then and the glow of the Pepsi Machine on the porch of Midway diner was like a beacon.

Andy and I got out and snuck up to it. I shoved the mason jar into the trap door where the drinks fall and lit the long fuse that hung out. We ran like hell to the car and waited for eternity. Just as we started to wonder if the fuse had gone out, the whole door exploded off the front of the machine and an assortment of Pepsi-brand cokes sprayed into the air! We were MacGyver!

When I went to get the paper for dad the next morning, the headline read: "LOCAL BOMBER STRIKES!" They actually had pictures of shrapnel and a couple of the mailboxes. For the Southside Gankin' Posse, this was our first publicity and I was proud. I started my own little parade down the driveway until I saw words FELONY and FEDERAL crimes. To me, it was just a mailbox. Sure, I figured if we got caught, we would get punished, but it NEVER occurred to me that bombing mailboxes may wind the posse up in prison! In days to come, more reports of bombed mailboxes rolled in and we were yet another headline. "BOMBER STRIKES AGAIN". They even went on to tell how thorough they intended to investigate due to the danger and severity of the crime. They found one mailbox on the entire other side of the road!

With that much talk in a town so small, I knew we would get caught. I imagined the cops busting down the door and carting me off to rot for good. That would have been better than what did happen. Remember mom said everyone called dad *Killer*? Well, that's who came and yanked me up! I was scooping ice cream at the VFW stand at the horse show. (Shelbyville is the Walking Horse Capital of the World and hosts the annual Celebration. It was a big money-maker for our town for years and organizations in town had booths for fundraisers.) It sucked because it was hot as hell, but it was awesome, because, well, it was ice cream. I liked to hook my friends up when they came through. Anyway, that's where I was when my dad stormed in with actual fire in his eyes. All he said was, "John Boy, come with me NOW." I knew I was in some deep shit.

We walked with over a car length between us and he didn't speak a word. We got in the car and he drove me to the police station and made me go in alone. A bunch of detectives interrogated me and tried to tell me that my friend had ratted me out. But the Southside Gankin' Posse doesn't believe in snitching and loyalty was number one. I let those detectives know I didn't know what they were talking about.

> **Andy:** I had just gotten home from Opryland and my stepsister said, "Hey, the Sheriff was here looking for you, and wants you to come down to the station as soon as you get back." I was immediately scared to death. My mom took

me down there. They were already questioning Smo about the bombs in another interrogation room. He was playing dumb, and I denied it all as well.

A lack of confession didn't matter in the end because they found plenty of evidence when the police searched my room. They found my tacklebox with black powder residue and bottle rocket fuses. Busted! They also found the guy who bought us the gun powder. He didn't own a muzzle loader, so his purchase was suspicious. He obviously owed us no loyalty, so we were caught. They wound up charging us with FELONY manufacturing, processing, and transporting illegal bombs *and* blowing up Federal and Private property. My parents had to hire an attorney and pay for a brand-new Pepsi machine. That was definitely not cheap.

> **Andy:** We had to pay for everybody's mailboxes and go apologize to everyone individually. We were put on probation, and to top it all off, PEPSI SUED US for the cost of the cover of the machine!

Chapter 3:
The Hustler

Yeah, I been zip lock poppin' since I was a teenager
Independent hustle, still ballin' with the majors
Grindin' out the stix on the dirt road code
I came up from flippin' bricks to rockin' sold out shows
~ **Shake**

In seventh grade, we moved from the farm to a beautiful house on the Duck River. It was the dopest house for a teenager! The River House days are when I really became known as Smo. I had always tagged along with Chris even though he was a bit older than me, and I think they got a kick out of having the kid brother around. Chris had the nickname "Shmu" from a partying incident where that was literally the only sound he could create. It stuck and then I started getting called "Little Shmu". So from there it was always Shmo, and eventually it became Big Smo. Some of my teachers even called me Smo instead of John. It just became a thing and now here we are.

The River House move was ideal for my teenage years. I got along with everybody PLUS I had a super cool crib, so my house became the place to be. So many people would come hang out and I would entertain.

I cooked at the country club while I was still on probation and I had gotten really good at making food. Of course mom cooked enough for a small army every day, so there was always plenty. It was an open invitation and we just really did whatever we wanted.

> **Momma Smo:** We converted the garage into a bedroom. Chris joined the service about that time, so John had the whole downstairs to himself. Thank God I didn't have to listen to and see all the people that came back and forth through there. I'll run into people now who say, "Oh, I used to come to your house," and my reply is, "You did?" I sure heard about a lot of people being at my house, and I didn't know anything about it!

> **Andy:** We came in whenever we wanted, and I mean, it could be 3 in the morning and they had a little kitchenette downstairs. His mom would leave a note saying, "Make sure you eat before you go to bed," and there would be a hot pot of chili on the stove just waiting on us. We would just sit around, eat chili, and hang until the sun came up.

Hangin with my cat Dominique

Let me tell you one of my favorite stories from the River House. Now, I know my parents weren't stupid, but we did manage to get away with A LOT and we definitely partied at that house. Neither of my parents did "drugs", but my dad sure did enjoy his nasty Moore cigars. One day I popped into the garage and my dad was watching golf on TV from his golf cart. It smelled like WEED! He was so chill sitting there and I noticed it definitely was not one of his Moores in the ashtray – it was a blunt! Somehow, we had managed to leave behind a party favor and my dad got a hold of it. He said, "Run down to the store and get us steaks. I want to grill out!" I drove to the store thinking, "Holy shit, my dad has the munchies." We never told him.

Moving to the River House had a huge impact on me. Before we moved, my school had been all country kids. When I moved to town, my school was much more diverse. So now I knew the country kids and the city kids. By the time I made it to high school, I knew everybody in town. I liked to spend my lunch time at school designing different haircuts. Linda at the beauty shop had done my hair since I was a kid and she (and thankfully my parents too) were willing to let me try any kind of crazy hair from braids to designs. She shaved "Ice, Ice Baby" in one side one week and then a spider web the next. Every week I'd have a new design for Linda.

> **Momma Smo:** I never knew what he was going to come back looking like. He really had "*Ice, Ice Baby*" carved in his hair. You name it, and they did it. My husband and I figured, "Hell with it."

> **Tommy:** Smo has always been a rapper! When he was in Junior High, he was always rapping and stuck out. He just had that style.

Andy: He could make a room brighten up when he walked into it – even as kids. Everybody in the room was drawn to him. I've never seen anybody like that ever.

I went to a typical high school with the usual groups of kids. I just hung out with everyone and my fashion taste was just what I liked. I loved the styles of my idols and I imitated their style with my own little twist. I even liked to create my own "pieces". Remember the Gankin' Posse shirts? Well, I went back to my airbrush guy on more than one occasion to get his help creating my signature designs. My favorite pair of pants from my collection were jeans with a hole in the leg. I painted my brother's crew, the *8 Ball Posse*, onto different fabric. I sewed their logo into the hole so that the 8-ball showed. Hip hop and the culture were my greatest influences during my later teen fashion years. My class ring was huge and gold with a green stone. On top of the stone was a gold money sign and on one side, a low rider truck. The continent of Africa was on the other. (It probably wound up at a pawn shop in Shelbyville. Ha!) My unique style definitely didn't go unnoticed-I got the superlative for Most Stylish!

> **Momma Smo:** He would get a brand-new pair of pants or overalls and hang them on the clothesline and shoot it with a gun to make a hole. He was probably the first person to shoot holes in his pants! He always had to be different. That was stylish later on, but my son was the first one to do it at his school. He always was ahead of things.

The Undercover Lover, My First Car

Aside from my fashion sense, cars have always caught my eye. Much like my hair and clothes, I liked cars with a little more character. The first car I WANTED was a funeral hearse. My mom wouldn't have that, so we settled for a 1987 Chevy Celebrity station wagon with the words "Undercover Lover" across the windshield.

John Lee '94

Senior Year At SCHS

By the time I graduated, I traded the Celebrity for an Oldsmobile Silhouette Minivan. My buddies and I decided to take it to Gatlinburg for our Senior Trip. We took the seats out and put a speaker in the middle of the floor for entertainment and a foot rest. The drive should only have taken a few hours but instead took about ten! We rode the van up and down the strip for hours with the door wide open. My favorite memory from that trip was when I decided to bungee jump! I'm terrified of heights, so that was a real thrill for me! That was one of the best trips I've been on to this day!

Reality set in after graduation, and I decided to go to bar tending school. It was an excellent fit for me because it seemed to be the perfect combo of business and pleasure! I already had a handle on the kitchen and was quite the chef by this point. I thought maybe I could even bartend at the country club one day. I took my "training" so seriously, that I had a fully stocked bar at the River House and would practice on my friends. We can all imagine how that turned out. In the end, I was an excellent bar tender, but a horrible student. You can probably assume from my interests and lack of mention of my academic achievements, I just wasn't the star pupil. That trend would follow me for years in spite of how much I love to write, rhyme, and create.

I really wasn't a good student and, for me, school was about socializing. Band and drama class are probably the only courses I took seriously after about fourth grade. I went to high school and participated, but I was definitely never on the honor roll. I know my parents were so relieved when I got my diploma. After graduation, I started a journey to try and find out who I was professionally speaking. Here's a short list of some of the attempted and ultimately failed paths of study or potential careers I pursued:

- Electrician – too much math

- Drafting – more math than electrician (back to square one)

- Machinery – that just wasn't for me

- Truck Driving – passing a drug test may be a problem. We also determined during that period of my life that I have sleep apnea and couldn't stay awake driving for long periods of time. That ruined that chance.

- Body Snatcher with Andy – he worked at the funeral home. That's all I'll speak on that job.

- Barber School – too many chemicals for my bad skin (I'll explain)

- Concrete – the hardest yet most rewarding job I've worked. I wrote a lot of rhymes watching concrete dry all over my town.

- Hustler – Pro: made a lot of money, Con: illegal

> **Momma Smo:** We spent so much money on that kid. My husband put him in the 18-wheeler driving course and he couldn't drive. He'd go to sleep, and one of his friends told us, "John snores really bad." In high school, his bedroom was downstairs so we couldn't hear it, but we took him to the doctor and sure enough, he had sleep apnea, so he couldn't drive a truck. Then he went to Nashville to Electronics school and we spent a lot of money there.

I have had two obstacles in life that seem to always interfere with my professional success. The first is my skin, and the second is, well, drug tests. Sadly, my skin is the reason for not being able to pass a drug test. Let me explain. When I was around eleven, I started to have excruciating pain and itching. It was "poison ivy" to some doctors and "an allergic reaction" to others. All the while, chunks of my skin were falling off and over eighty percent of my body had raw open wounds. Needless to say this was painful and of course embarrassing. I know a lot of people comment on how outgoing and friendly I was as a kid, but in reality, it was not easy to deal with a disease that everyone can SEE! My condition made me angry and reclusive at times (that, and because I was a kid on probation!) and that's what lead me to start writing. I spent a lot of time alone and miserable in my early teen years and it got to me.

Writing really helped me through those times. We continued to go to doctor after doctor to find a solution and some relief. In the most unexpected way, I met the best medicine for my problem. Like I said, Chris and his buddies always let me come along. They would even let me party with them when I was way younger. It seemed like a funny idea to get "Little Shmu" high, so I went along with it. That little bit of pot and I had instant relief. Sometimes I think people are shocked to know that I am an advocate for cannabis research and medicinal use. Everyone thinks I'm just about cedar pine for a good time, but I will tell you that from the day I was introduced to marijuana, I have found no other medicine that cures what ails me like she does. That being said, I started my cannabis journey at a very young age. After that first time, I became a big fan of Mary Jane (and I don't mean my mom! Ha!)

My first job was working at the pencil factory in town. I would leave high school and work half the day there. I showed up with bandages and someone asked what was wrong. By this age, I was used to the shocked looks and gaping mouths. Immediately I was let go because it was a health hazard to be around so much lead with raw skin. I got fired from food service and turned away from interviews. I felt like a failure and, on top of that, I was in so much pain! I thought I would never be successful, but I was spending a lot more time with Tyrone. I learned that no one in the dope game cares about my skin. Slowly but surely, I was making LOTS of money!

I tried all the jobs and trades that my dad suggested (and funded), but they just weren't for me. It dawned on me one day that I should try something that I was passionate about! I would go to barber school. Now, my skin problems began when I was eleven, so I now had over a decade of dealing with my condition. At one point I thought I might lose the outer part of my ear because it had gotten so bad. I wrapped myself in cloth diapers because the bandages had become so costly. Each week I got cortisone shots to try to help, and of course, I just kept on toking. So here I am wanting to go to barber school with this going on with my body.

Barber School was interesting

Momma Smo: He was going to Barber School, and when he interacted with the chemicals there, his skin would break out and he had to quit. He had a skin problem, it was pitiful. His hands looked like someone ripped all of his skin off. It was just red, raw and he couldn't stand water to touch it, and couldn't stand to sit really. He was on disability for several years because every time he would try a job, his skin would act up. He worked at 2 country clubs in the kitchen until he got involved with some kind of chemical and would break out and would have to quit that job.

It wasn't long after starting barber school that my skin took a turn for the worst. I couldn't have my hands in chemicals and water all day. I felt defeated and it made me angry. I decided to hell with school. I wanted to make money. Tyrone had a spare bedroom in Murfreesboro, so I went to live with him. We pooled our resources and hit the ground running as a team. I want you to understand, I don't want anyone to think I was out selling drugs because it was easy money. I was a young guy and I wanted to provide for and take care of myself. I wanted to prove it to everyone. That pride coupled with so many failures motivated me to be a real hustler.

My 21st Birthday Party!

> **Andy:** Tyrone taught us everything about hustling. He was older than us, and could get you whatever you wanted, and that's what he did for a living. At first it was fun, we were all grinding and had a good hook-up through Tyrone, so we were making great money.

> **Tyrone:** We had more than one apartment, one for this and one for that. Right outside on the porch we had a camera with a mic. Now we could see and hear anyone when they pulled up outside our door.

My new job was pretty easy because we lived in the largest college town in the state. Demand was definitely higher than supply, so we were AL-WAYS busy. Our apartment was a fortress. Now being young dudes in a dangerous profession (or maybe it was paranoia), we took our home security very seriously. We had a kick-proof door, surveillance cameras, and an arsenal. One night our door was getting kicked and Tyrone flipped on the TV to see the outside cameras. Outside three guys with ski masks were standing there trying to rob us. They kicked and kicked, but never got in. They took off and we followed them, but never caught up. The next time someone kicked on our door, we weren't so lucky.

> **Tyrone:** I'll never forget because there was a tornado coming through Murfreesboro. I remember when the cops got to the door, they came in and said, "Yeah, we know about this apartment."

I woke up being shaken by a cop asking me where the dope was. They tossed the room and only found some stems and seeds, so I ended getting a simple possession charge. We might could have gotten away with it until they brought out the K-9 dog. The second I saw the German Shepherd let itself out of the patrol car and waltz right in our apartment without a leash, we were screwed. Big time. Sure enough they found

Tyrone's stash in the vacuum cleaner and we both got charged. Tyrone protested it was his and that I shouldn't be charged, but they put us both in cuffs and drove us straight to 940 for booking.

My dad came not too long after I called him. He told the officer that he would be bailing us both out. I remember the cop thought my dad was only there for me, but he learned quickly that Killer showed up for the duo.

> **Tyrone:** When we got arrested in Murfreesboro, his dad came down to get us, and I think our bonds were like $35,000 each. I had access to the money, I just didn't have it with me there, so his dad comes down and says, "Yeah, I'm gonna get them out," and I'll never forget, the officer calls him to the side and says, "The black guy too?" Aw man, Carl lost it, and yelled, "Where's your superior? Hell yes, the BLACK GUY TOO!" He was wild with it, "I can't believe this shit... 'The black guy too?' Get them out of there, both of them, I want them out of there right now and I want to see your superior." I said, "Mr. Carl, let's just go, it's all good," and he said, "No, I want to talk to somebody, because that doesn't make any sense."
>
> On the ride back to our apartment, he was hot, "I can't believe that guy, 'The black guy too...'" He just kept saying that over and over, it seemed like he was more pissed about that than us being arrested. When we got back to our apartment, he said, "Okay, guys, you're on the radar now, so I want you out of here. Pack your stuff." We both moved back to the River House.

Tyrone stayed with me at the River House after the arrest and we hired the same attorney. Oddly enough, my skin condition wound up being the reason I didn't have to serve jail time, but I did get my probation majorly extended. I would have been a liability in jail because of the weeping wounds, and they decided it was best for me to serve my punishment at home. Even crazier, the medication that I was on for my skin caused a false positive for marijuana, so I basically didn't have to worry about passing a drug test anymore.

In an attempt to make amends for getting arrested, I tried one more futile attempt to go back to school. This time, technology! I started ITT Tech in Nashville and met a whole new group of clientele. I was doing a lot of traveling back and forth between Nashville and the River House for school, so I needed a hub to work out of. I managed to get connected with the front desk guy at the Stadium Inn that worked with me to keep customers flowing out of the old abandoned Elvis Suite all night. I wasn't learning much about technology, but I was definitely supplying clients in over three counties.

My Good Friend JJ

JJ: I first met Smo at ITT Tech in Nashville. We had to stand up and introduce ourselves. When it was Smo's turn, and I'll never forget, he stood up in a basketball jersey and shorts, with a chain around his neck, and platinum corn rows with a silver briefcase at his side, and said "I'm John Lee Smith, I'm 26 years old and I'm here to make my father happy. I've been to barber school and done a few other things, and I guess that's kind of my story," and sat back down. My buddies looked at each other like, "Yeah, this dude's a dealer!" I've known him 20 years now!

While I was "going to school," I had to work another job to get by. Also, I needed a cover for how I had so much money in the first place. I loved cutting hair even though it was so painful. I was still cutting my homies' hair because they knew that it wasn't contagious which is so hard to get people to understand when you have a skin condition. If you have one, I know your pain! Hang in there! I was really good at it, but it was becoming unbearable. The dermatologist finally said, "I prohibit you from doing this job, and basically any other one that exposes your skin!" That's how my laborious, expensive, stressful, and downright horrible quest for disability benefits began. Sadly, if anyone knows anything about a painful skin condition, there's a lot more than just itchy skin-there's anger, depression, anxiety, humiliation, aggravation, irritability, you get it. I was a joy to be around back then! If anyone knows anything about being a man in his early twenties, the disability office is one of the last places you want to be. I was in a low place in those days. As shameful as it is, (yet probably so true in too many disability cases), I turned outlaw to earn money to AFFORD to get on disability. By this time I had mouths to feed, and I needed to make money even if I couldn't "get" a job.

In my line of work, the last place you want to wind up is in court and by this point, I had been there too many times. I had to defend my disability case to the judge and after too much rigmarole and frustration, I lost it. For those of you that know me personally, you know I have a hot temper when the fuse gets lit just right, especially back in my earlier years. I said some choice words to the judge. Think NWA style but replace "the police" with "you, Judge". Little did I know that the United States government considers that choice phrase specifically a "threat to a *Federal Judge*".

Imagine a US Marshall calling you with that news. Stress and struggle are the two biggest triggers for a hellacious flare up. I was miserable. I guess that call was the last straw because I just told that stranger on the other line every single hardship and heartache I had survived since I was a kid. I didn't tell a sob story to get out of getting in trouble, but I had a stranger on the line who was my last chance. I couldn't go down without a fight. That tenacity paid off on more than one occasion in my life, and at that moment I knew this man had to understand how desperate I was. I guess it struck a nerve with him because I ended up just getting a warning.

Now I should add another layer of complication to the situation because my desperation was most powerfully fueled by my responsibility to my daughter. I found out I would be Ameria's daddy when I was only twenty-three, and it was hard to know I was about to become a dad when I wasn't nearly at the place my parents had been when I was born. I wanted to provide for my family, but I still relied so heavily on my own parents. I'm so thankful for their support through those early years. One of my favorite photos is of my dad and me when I held Ameria for one of the first times! I love this picture of us! Ameria was really close to my parents and I'm thankful she and my dad had that time together. My mom's influence on Ameria has been so incredibly strong, she's been nicknamed Granny Mer-Mer because she's a mini Mary Jane. (Actually Ameria *and* Lanica are mini Mary Janes!)

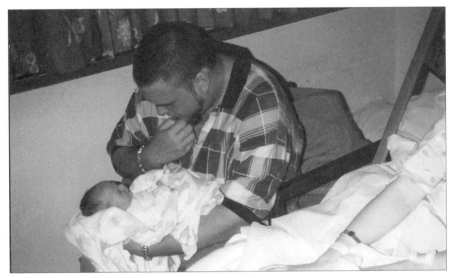

Ameria, Born 2-15-99

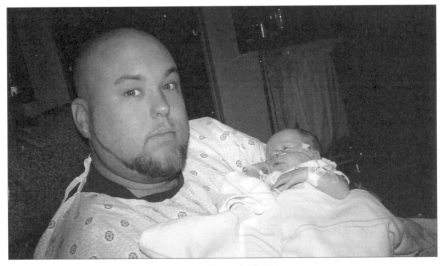

Lanica, Born 4-23-03

Needless to say, I had put my folks through the ringer. With the disability benefits, I was able to provide the necessities for my family so that I could quit cutting hair. I worked odd construction and cash jobs for buddies, and all the while, I kept the Elvis suite at the top of the Stadium Inn rockin' with business. ITT Tech didn't pan out, but I had met JJ and he was now part of my team.

After I moved back to the River House, I linked up with some old buddies of mine that were into music. I was laying low a lot more, and since I was back home, I had a lot more time to write. My buddy Adam Cataldo had an apartment with a studio in Wartrace. He had a drum machine and an 8-track Tascam recorder. I was fascinated by them, so he said I could take them home and mess with them. Once I got them set up, I connected a Radio Shack microphone and some of my dad's headphones. That's when I wrote one of my first raps, *The Dope Game*.

Chapter 4:
Now We're Cookin'

It's the weekend at the Kuntry Kitchen
Got a grill full'a food with the southern fixins'
~ Honky Tonkin'

Orig the DJ: I was in 8th grade, and my friend Benji Burris and I were walking to school one day and saw Smo driving his car down the road. He was in this low-rider with tinted windows and had this crazy bleach-blonde hair, he was this total character! Benji said, "Yeah, that's my cousin Shmo," Fast forward 2 years later at a party when I was in 10th grade. We wound up hanging out at a party and from there, we started hanging out, and hitting back roads together, just kicking it.

I was a DJ, so we would work on music when we hung out. I already had the whole set up in my bedroom. I had maybe 10 cool Hip-Hop records, like Cypress Hill, Kriss Kross, DJ Jazzy Jeff, and the Fresh Prince. Everything else was Mozart or some weird unknown country artist from the 60s, and I was looping those, and then making drum beats with the 707. Smo showed up with Adam's drum machine and wanted my help. He had written some poetry by then, but he'd never really rapped on a record yet. He'd been listening to rap music for years and had the style of a rapper already and wanted to put his poetry to music. I figured out the drum machine and we were in business!

At first, we were digging our music and our close friends were into it, but Smo hadn't found his tone yet. Back then, Haystak was a big influence in the style of music we were listening to. It was hood, dirty South rap we were doing, but West Coast influenced, but this was WAY before Country Rap. So at the time, we were just imitating Haystak and Trick Daddy and Eminem, just trying to make beats like that and follow in those footsteps.

Orig is one of the best people I have had in my life, especially during those times. We were instant best friends, musical soul mates. It was like whatever one of us lacked, the other made up for it. We made awesome music together. Crazy enough, his dad was also a career Navy guy, and we were born at the same hospital in San Diego. I loved Orig's family too. With Orig, it wasn't about partying. We were working. Orig probably kept me out of prison. I honestly believe I would have never discovered my talent without him. He was a positive influence on me in a time when I really needed somebody.

> **Orig the DJ:** I knew at that time Smo was getting into a lot of trouble with the law. When he met me, his troubles started to kind of go away because he was focusing more on music. I was really focused on music at an earlier age, so I didn't get into the kinds of run-ins with the law that Smo did because I was always in my room working on beats. Then when I met him, we started doing that together and it became more important than anything else to both of us.

The Old Farm House

We copied *The Dope Game* on cassettes and took it with us everywhere. It motivated us to work on more beats. The first people I gave my tape away to were some hippies on a camping trip at Fall Creek Falls. I played the tape and they didn't believe it was me! Enough people seemed to like our music and we had found our rhythm. We decided it was time to get serious.

By this time, I had moved where I actually live today. We had the studio set up in the house and it just got to be too much. Now where I live is my mom's family farm and on the side of the property is an old building. Back in the 1890s up until the 1940s, the building was an operating store. At first, we just used the building as a smoke shack because it hadn't been cleaned out in years. It actually kinda smelled stale and like dead mice now that I think back on it. Well, we decided it would be the perfect spot to relocate the studio! I asked my dad for help because he was an electrician in the Navy and had a knack for carpentry. He did all the wiring and built out the control room and the vocal booth. We had so much fun building the studio together. It was like the old Pinewood Derby days. One day, we were working on the vocal booth and he suddenly drew up like he was having a muscle spasm and rushed out of the room. He said, "Follow me. We're going to the hospital." He just jumped in his El Camino and peeled out. I really didn't know what was going on, but I followed him. He got down the highway a bit and I noticed he was slumped down in his seat. It scared me to death, so I pulled up beside him and yelled, "What the hell is the matter with you?" He said, "I dropped my cigarettes!" Once we got to the hospital, the apparent "stroke" was just a fat boy cramp! He helped from start to finish.

Kuntry Kitchen studio

After a few months, we were done. We decided the most appropriate way to celebrate the grand opening was to have a huge party in the field. The newly renovated building was the "VIP" room that people paid to hang out in. I definitely remember Chris Yancy got naked that night and I flipped a golf cart. That should tell you what kind of night it was!

We named it the "Kuntry Kitchen". Now, I had the plug on having a place to record music. I had been to another home studio in town a while back and knew that there weren't many local spots to record. Orig and I had already been to Missouri and had a horrible experience at a studio, not to mention lost a lot of money. We had a crew by this point that we were making music with and we needed money to fund our project, so we decided to establish Yayoda Records. People came from all over and we were making a lot of bread doing studio sessions. In between sessions, we worked on our own project. Orig went to school to become a producer and sound engineer during the day while I poured concrete. In the evening, we would grill out and work all night long.

Orig would show me everything that he learned in class. We literally learned as we went. The studio had a couple of couches and we would write and make beats, jump in and record, then straight to the next song. It was complicated, but we learned so much during that process.

> **Orig the DJ:** We weren't really aiming for a sound on *Kuntry Kitchen*, we were just making sounds and exploring the possibilities and our limits of what we could do. We were very creative so that process just happened organically. That album was my first attempt at really mixing and mastering, and actually making a CD.

My dad was supportive through the whole thing. He seemed proud to see me follow the project through. I even dedicated the second track title *Killa* for him. The entire thing took about three years to create.

Orig the DJ: Smo's dad was one of the greatest people I've ever known. He definitely was supporting everything Smo was doing musically because it kept us out of trouble and gave us something to work towards. We had a marker board in the studio where we put up our goals and would check them off. Killer was proud.

We were doing live performances at the VFW while we were working on the album. Everything started to be a little too much to juggle, so I reached out to Chris for some help. He designed our artwork and helped with distribution. He was a huge help and always has been since! We needed an investor, so I used some connections from my dealings in the hustle to fund getting the album pressed. From there, Chris got us into stores, and we were finally being heard!

Orig the DJ: His brother Chris was actually the Executive Producer of *Kuntry Kitchen* because he helped us come up with the game plan of getting CDs made, and said to us, "Why don't you guys put your money where your mouth is and take some of your best works and make an actual, tangible product?" So that's where he pushed us to have direction. He came out with his camera, and knew a little bit about Photoshop, and helped us put together the album cover art.

Chris: I was the Photoshop guy, so I could do the artwork graphics and we collaborated to build the album graphics the way it is on the CD.

Once we had CDs, we had a product to push, and I was an excellent salesman. We sold them out of the trunk in Nashville and put them in consignment smoke shops around town. We had CDs at the local corner store and at my buddy Rodney Yoe's barber shop. My stuff is still on sale there today. Thanks, Rodney.

JJ: It's true, when the *Kuntry Kitchen* album was out, we used to go down to the street corners in Nashville and sell them for a couple dollars if we could.

After selling so many CDs, we started performing more. We would perform for anyone that would listen. One of our first shows was on Halloween night at the annual Jaycee's haunted house. We had smoke bombs, strobe lights, and tons of people. It was also the first time my parents saw us perform! It was awesome!

Andy: After the haunted house opening, we threw a party at my house and he put on a show in my backyard. We probably had 300 people there. He got all these other rap acts from Nashville, Columbia, and Franklin who came to my house to see the show.

The Halloween performance had gone so well that we decided to pay the $50 entry into the Shelbyville Christmas parade. My dad lent us a trailer and helped us construct our float which was really more like a moving stage. My mom made a Santa suit out of sweatpants, a hoodie, and some fur. We performed our first ever Christmas song, *All I Want for Christmas is My 6 Gold Teeth* a total of forty-six times during the length of the parade. That song can be found on YouTube under *Ghetto Christmas*. Go look it up. I loved that my family was a part of the whole thing. The next morning we were on the cover of the paper.

Orig the DJ: Killer was very supportive in every aspect of Smo's music. He helped us build backdrops, and when we did that Christmas parade, I drew characters on wood, and he cut them out and secured them onto a trailer he let us borrow. He even let us borrow his truck to tow it on. He'd do anything for Smo.

Front Page with the Christmas Parade

I had started to gain some recognition in the rap game, but that didn't slow the hustling. On top of that my dad was diagnosed with lung cancer. I had a family and bills, so I worked any job I could get my hands on. I started pouring concrete with a good friend of mine, Travis Edwards. He was also the lead singer of a heavy metal band called Ballistic Whiplash. He let us open for them, and their fans were great! I learned a lot watching him perform and we loved the exposure!

While Orig was at SAE school in Nashville, we found out his instructor was the MC at Kung Fu Coffee on 4th Avenue in Nashville. We paid $40 for a 15-minute spot and to put my face on the flyer. At first, the crowd didn't seem to know what to think of me, but we got a lot of compliments that night. We shared our CDs all over Nashville and even went to the hip hop station in town for support, but they turned us away. We knew we needed to get on the radio, but we just didn't know how that was going to happen. At my house we picked up a hip hop and R&B station in Athens, Alabama. We figured we would give it a shot, so we made a dope advertisement using our music to announce an event we had coming up. We purchased some airtime in a commercial slot, and they liked our style so much, they reached out to us. They had a DJ that needed some drops done, so we made some sixty second intros for his set. Shout out to DJ LIL-D at 93.3 in Athens for all the love!

Around that same time, Orig and I met some dudes in Nashville and we started making music with them. Even though we lived in the country and they lived in the city, we had plenty in common. We laughed about writing gangster rap in a cornfield and kept experimenting with beats and my tone. Together, we began the work on my first solo album, *The True South*. Pay attention when you listen to the album. We did all the voices and created the fake radio station sounds. Orig taught me so much as we tinkered with sounds and instruments.

> **Orig the DJ:** In 2003, after *Kuntry Kitchen* came out, we met some guys in Nashville and put together a group called The Bushes Boys, which consisted of Smo, 6'5, and Lil Nitty and The Hitman, and then on the production side, 88 Keys, C-Note, and me. They were already making beats and doing battles in Nashville, and we all joined forces and became a killer trio. Smo had a more urban hip hop battle-type of delivery and, working with other rappers and producers, we were getting better. C-Note, 88 Keys, and I made a beat together that wound up being the beat for *Kuntry Livin'*. That's the first "hick hop" type of beat we ever did. They were actually making fun of the country, because these guys were from Nashville and they'd come all the way out to the middle of nowhere to make music.

While Orig was at school, I worked on the album and recorded people to make some side money. We worked on the project when we could, and between pouring concrete and working on music, I was going nonstop.

Orig the DJ: Everything we were doing was completely independent and underground. We threw a release party and held a meet and greet at Hastings to sign our album. Smo was always a marketing genius. He was the one with the game plan.

Once the album was done, we had to find a way to distribute our record. We didn't have luck at any of the bigger names, but luckily, Hastings in Murfreesboro and Tullahoma let us sell our music there! At several points throughout my career, Hastings was kind enough to sell my music and my mom's cookbooks. Sadly, it won't be around to sell this book. RIP Hastings. Thanks for all the support!

Orig the DJ: I paid a company to master the record and had already sent the mixes off to them when I found out Smo had already set a release date before we were going to have the masters back. We had to do the masters ourselves. It took us 3 days, and we literally did not sleep. We would master a song, burn it to a disc, listen to it on the truck speakers, take notes, then go back and fix whatever changes we thought. After those three days, we were so excited but EXHAUSTED. Three months later we got the masters back that we had professionally done, and ours sounded better! Looking back and comparing *Kuntry Kitchen* to *The True South*, to me it was a HUGE step forward, and that album is definitely a milestone in both my and Smo's Journey.

When I look back on the *Kuntry Kitchen* and *True South* days, it's like being a freshman in high school. We were excited and eager, but still so young and inexperienced. Sometimes though, I miss those days because we had so much freedom and creativity.

Part II:

NO TURNING BACK

Chapter 5:
The Graduate

I woke up this morning, tied my boots up
Because I knew it was gonna be a long day
~ Workin'

Back in the late 1990s, I worked security at the Mix Factory. It was a really popular club in Nashville during that time and it had a pretty rowdy crowd. My job was delivering drunk people out the front doors to the police. Little did I know, that security gig prepared me for how to deal with drunk fans when I'm on stage now. Eventually, I worked my way up to VIP security and happened to catch a glimpse of Haystak hanging out. By this point I was a big fan and admired what he was doing. I saw him live at Stampede back in 2000 but didn't get the chance to meet him until I reached out to his people to try to get him for a feature.

Now, I would like to remind everyone that I never called myself a country rapper, I'm just a rapper that grew up in the country. I worked with anyone I thought was talented. This crew of really young gangster dudes in Nashville reached out to me and asked me to film a documentary. Think six months of following street dudes around hustling in the city. We had a rule that if we were filming guns, they couldn't be loaded.

They put the ammo in their pants and when they aimed their guns and jumped toward the camera (and me), you could hear the tink of the bullets in their pockets!

I spent countless hours filming and editing the documentary and learned so much through the process. I really enjoyed it and was getting pretty good, so I was stoked when I saw a "Make Your Own Scary Movie" contest on Good Morning America. Since Andy and I have been horror movie buddies for forever, we decided to write a short film based on "The Mackenzies" from John Carpenter's *Halloween.* Jamie Lee Curtis' character tells the kids to run to the Mackenzies for help when Michael Myers is chasing them. In our film, campers are attacked and run through a cornfield for help. They knock on the door of the Mackenzies who turn out to be cannibals! Plot twist! We had so much fun making the film. Orig played the main role and we even made the film score! We didn't win the contest, but we learned so much about acting and editing. GMA, if you'd like to discuss the book or check out *The Mackenzies,* just let me know!

> **Andy:** My mom and step-dad actually played the Mackenzies.

Orig and I enjoyed incorporating the film aspect into our projects, so we decided to just film everything we did. I have boxes full of tapes from back in those days. By that time I could produce a cheap music video pretty quick, so I looked at it as easy money. I was hired to film a segment at the 2007 Nashville Hip Hop Awards for the rapper Lil Blaze. I found out that they were in contact with Haystak, so I asked them to reach out for a feature.

Me & my boy A2B doin what we do best... Clownin

Haystak showed up to the studio in a Suburban with an entourage. We chopped it up on the front porch of the studio for a bit and then he hopped in the booth. He basically free-styled the feature, listening and recording a line at a time. I was a big fan by this point of Stak's career, so I took note of everything he did that day. He was impressed by *The True South* album and all the digital work I was capable of. We hit it off instantly and he let me know that he would be in touch if he needed me to do any work for him. Little did I know that day would change the rest of my life.

Three days later I loaded all my gear in the back of my Ford Escort station wagon and took off on the nine-hour trek to Augusta, Georgia to film for him. We had a great time on that trip, and I was excited to get to play such a key role. After Augusta, I thought it would be cool if we did a show in my hometown. He could be the headliner and I would open for him. The show sold out and we nearly tore the house down. It was an awesome show and we even performed the song *Raised in the South* that we recorded at my house the first day we met. Not long after that, Stak asked would I go with him on tour to help out.

Smo and Stak

Haystak: I'm proud of Smo because he's an alumnus of Haystak U and he's proud of it. I first met him on January 8th, 2008. I remember that because it was a week after New Year's. Smo showed me some work he had done, and I was impressed. I was like, "Hey, how about this: You shoot videos for me, and do visuals for me," and he was all over it. I told him, "Here's the thing: it's not the greatest paying job, but I'll pay you something and let you sell your own brand of merchandise to my crowd.

The job was a 32-date tour being Stak's hype man as the opening act for the Insane Clown Posse's Dark Lotus tour in 2009. "Hype Man" is a very loose term to describe my job duties with Haystak. He's a particular guy and expects things to be a certain way, so I learned very quickly what he preferred and how to provide for him so the tour went smoothly. Basically, I just helped him out however he needed. While Stak napped before a show, I made sure to get his standard Wendy's order: 2 double stacks, 2 large fries, and a large Diet Mountain Dew. I'd put a couple of fresh packs of his favorite smokes on his bedside table and sit all the food in front his fan by his bunk. He would wake up happy and ready to perform. Some of my other tasks were doing laundry, cleaning the bus, and getting towels and water ready for the show.

I poked holes in water bottles so we could squirt them in our mouths for a drink or on the crowd for effect. They always loved that, and I still use that trick in my own shows today. I cannot begin to list all the things I learned during the three and a half years I worked for Haystak, but I'll share some of the most important. First of all, I learned how to do sound check. Over time, I had gotten good enough with knowing how Stak wanted us to sound so he just turned sound check over to me and went and did more important things. I also learned it's easier to sign someone's shirt if you tell them to turn around and use their back. Sounds simple but it's a lifesaver when you don't have a merch table.

> **Haystak:** You know, Smo watched everything I did when he was first out on the road with me, and I was very serious with him. He saw that it wasn't a game and learned fast!

We had a lot of fun on that tour and I was eager because I was experiencing things in the industry I had never gotten to see before. I had never traveled on a tour bus, so I learned the good and bad of that life. I tried to learn all the jobs on the tour because I dreamed that one day, I would have my own. I dove right in willing to do everything. Quickly I learned that ICP has a VERY loyal fan following. They are hard to impress, so we knew we only had the first 30 seconds of Stak's set to win their favor or we would be doused in all flavors of Faygo. We wrote a banger in the Kuntry Kitchen with their fans in mind, and luckily, at most shows it paid off. Obviously pretty much all of the crowd had come to see them, but slowly we were gaining fans.

> **Haystak:** I'll never forget, we were microphones 6 and 7, and these audiences didn't want to see us. So to go out in front of a thousand people and on the Eastern Seaboard in Baltimore, we might have 5, 10 fans in the house and we had to convert them every night.

You know, Smo watched everything I did when he was first out on the road with me, and I was very serious with him. He saw that it wasn't a game and learned fast! With Smo, he didn't do cowboy boots. He had his own style and it worked. Timberland-style work boots, jeans, t-shirt-that's what Smo was doing when I met him. I said, "That's the look," and he stayed with that formula. That was a big chance for him to take too, because when I first met him, Smo had a lot invested in another style of rap that was more street/gangster style, so it was a big gamble for him. I was a hard guy to work for, but Smo got the concept and we worked well together.

We had the same preshow routine I still do today: mic check, outfit check, and vocal warm up. It was an incredible experience sharing the stage with Stak. I was performing for the biggest crowds I'd ever stepped foot in front of. It was humbling to say the least, but it was also so exciting! We were totally in sync on stage and the crowd loved our energy. Over the course of the tour, I really grew as a performer and I'm still thankful to this day to have been given such an amazing opportunity.

After the 30-minute set, I sold merchandise and helped Stak with fans. He let me have a table to the side to sell *The True South* CDs and my own shirts. I really appreciate that Haystak was so willing to share his fan base and I'm thankful they were so receptive to my music. Stak even helped me create my first autograph back then: TN4-Big Smo.

The tour bus ran on bio-diesel, so another of my job duties was to siphon old grease from fast food restaurants in the middle of the night after shows. Sometimes the night crew would know about Haystak and would hook us up with food and give us the grease. Other times, we just had to find somewhere we could take it. So, one of my jobs was pumping fast food grease into a tour bus!

Being around other acts on the tour, I realized they had names for their fans. Stak had the CWBs and ICP had the Juggalos and Juggalettes. I was inspired and knew I needed to find a name for my fans, but I still wasn't sure what yet. We ended the tour in Nashville at a packed show at the Wildhorse Saloon. After the tour, I worked twice as hard on my own music. I used the momentum to create more content and I performed any chance I could.

Haystak had the idea to create a mini movie for his *Clinging to Life* project. The concept was to shoot Stak in a hospital fighting for his life from a gunshot wound. I reached out to some friends of mine who let us use the hospital, complete with Life Flight and real emergency staff. Stak let me create all the special effects and I shot the entire film. He trusted me a lot to try my own style and ideas and was an excellent test subject in my early film years. The movie turned out to be a success yet was never released; however, I'm still proud of that project today.

Three and a half years passed during the time I worked for Stak. We were traveling a lot and I was working on my own projects as well as the ones Stak and I were doing together. It had gotten to be a lot trying to be the opening act, the hype man, and the assistant, all the while trying to focus on being an artist myself. It was time to graduate from the University of Haystak.

> **Haystak:** Smo was becoming such an entity that the time came when we had become two different entities. Around me, he was always going to be a # 2 guy, and I wanted him to go and do his own thing. He did and made history.

Chapter 6:
American Roots

They wanna see what's on my mind
The stories that I tell
The heavens that I seek
While I'm livin' in this hell
Addicted to a state of mind
Fueled by the sells
To merchandise my life
And let me die up on a shelf
~ Old Dirt Road

After working for Haystak, I continued to put the finishing touches on the album I was working on called *American Made*. Myspace was popping for sharing music and collaborating with other people in the industry. I met a producer named Mr. Sneed from Ohio. During that time, he and some others were the ones that helped me discover what is now my signature sound. He was not only a talented rapper, but also very good at creating graphics with really impressive artwork. We did some trade work swapping feature spots on my tracks for graphic design ideas. One of the very first tracks that we worked on together was the first times the words *Boss of the Stix* were recorded out of my mouth. In those days I wasn't spending near as much time in the streets and my country lifestyle had only been exaggerated more by all the time I was spending at mud parks and performing for people like me. I was still just a rapper with a country sound and lyrics. Country rap wasn't anything anyone was really acknowledging as a genre. I said, "I'm the King of the Kuntry, The Boss of the Stix" and it just stuck. I had a chorus.

The idea to name the album *American Made* was to pay tribute to my dad. I did tons of shows at the VFW and had so many fans that were in the service. My music was starting to transform, and my lyrics celebrated my patriotism. I recognized it was time to focus on my brand and image and I wanted people to know what I stand for. I still had the issue of naming my fans. Sneed and I were on the phone one day brainstorming, when it just hit us. I said to Sneed, "How about Kinfoke?" We decided it was fitting and worth a try. It's crazy to think about how it grew to what it is today. I now have third and fourth generation Kinfoke and even fans with it tattooed on them! It's a family and I love my Kinfoke. #KF4L

> **Orig the DJ:** The biggest feedback we get from country listeners is, "You know, I don't really like rap, but I like this!"

> **Charlie Bonnet III:** I got a call from a friend asking if I wanted to make some money working for a rapper. I chuckled because I'd never collaborated with a rap artist before. I sang the hook on *Old Dirt Road* and sang and played guitar on *My Life in a Jar* and *American Made*.

During that same time, I met an East Coast producer named Jon Conner. He sent some beats to Stak, but they weren't the sound he was looking for at the time. Stak let JC know that I was more into Country and asked would it be OK if I gave them a listen.

Jon: I produced a total of 42 tracks for Haystak over a period of years. Smo was working for Haystak when we were doing the *Hard2Love* album. I sent Stak some beats that he said were too country for him, but that Smo might would like them. By 2009, the beats I sent had more country instrumentation. When Stak passed on those, Smo would put them into a folder for himself. One of those songs became *Kickin' It in Tennessee*.

I'll never forget the first time I listened to that beat. I said, "This is it right here!" Within minutes I had the chorus. I remember it so vividly because it was the most inspired writing session I've ever had. A friend was over and asked how I write a song. I explained that my motto is if I don't live it, I don't spit it. I said, "For instance, well we're just sittin' in the back yard blowin' pine, sippin' on that moonshine all the time." Then wide-eyed, I was like, "Holy shit that's it!" And then we just wrote the song. My buddy Relapse, a rapper from Atlanta, joined me later to co-write the classic anthem in exchange for music video production. (That's what we call the HOOK UP!)

Unfortunately during this time, I managed to wind up in Bedford County Jail for a simple possession marijuana charge. A week in jail in my hometown wound up being more like a high school reunion. I rapped for my cell block and the guards even bumped my music from my Myspace page. One night, I laid in my bunk and wrote *American Made*. To pass the time, my buddy Catfish and I worked on a song called *D Block* to pay homage to our time on the inside.

After that, I was contacted by some independent artists that needed a place to record a song with Lil Wyte from the Three 6 Mafia Camp. I told them to come on out and while they were here working, I let Lil Wyte check out some of my stuff I was working on. He heard the beat for *Kuntry Boys* and said he wanted to get on the track. Meanwhile, Jelly Roll showed up at the studio and said *he* wanted on the track too! So now, I had a song with Lil Wyte and Jelly Roll that was a banger. I was pumped to say the least. The guys that came to record had a show not too far from the studio, so they asked if I would mind earning some cash and filming their show. We piled up and rode out to Manchester in an ice storm to film a class act performance at Club Europa (who I also did promo advertising short clips for on the radio).

Making the video for *Kickin' It in Tennessee* came together as easily as the song had. We shot most of the video in a day. It only took about a month to put together everything that we had shot, and we were ready. At this time, we didn't promote our music or have release dates. I didn't really have a fan base waiting around for new music, so I was TRIP-PING when the video hit one million views. The comments kept rolling in and it was a lot to deal with. But of course, it was also awesome. This was exactly what we had worked so hard for! People were not only listening to us but seeing us too! One challenge for filming *Kickin' It in Tennessee* was that I needed to be in front of the camera and behind it at the same time. I got my buddy J.J. to be the camera guy and our other buddy Fat Pat to help him. I just said, "Keep the camera on me." We would shoot, I would watch the clip, and we would re-shoot or move on. Let's be honest, we were just having a good time with our friends, so it wasn't that hard.

> JJ: Smo needed somebody to film while he rapped, and that was maybe my first time ever touching a camera as far as shooting a video. So we shot all the video of him out on the river, out on the tractor, on the bridge with the truck, and out in the corn fields. Where he's sitting on the tractor,

this farmer named Carl Brown and his guys stopped what they were doing in the middle of farming and let us use their tractor!

Without a doubt, the most shocking part of that music video is when we chop the chicken's head off. It's a clip from another video that was removed from YouTube called "How to Kill a Chicken". It went through all the proper steps but chopping the head off with a Samurai sword was too graphic for some YouTube viewers. It's by far the most memorable moment of all my videos.

> **Tommy:** He called me in Florida when he told me he finally reached a million views. I cried because I was proud. It was incredible to watch it all happen. I was at his house after that and watched him pack up 1000 *American Made* CDs and autographed bandanas to send to troops in Iraq.
>
> He's the same now as he was then – doing charity shows and giving CDs away. He's always been that type of person and he still is today. That's what I love about him. He's the same John I've known since we were kids. When *American Made* came out is when stuff started to take off!

Before *Grassroots,* I worked on some other projects. Artists were connecting online and working together which made it possible for me to do a song with a group called Dubblewide in Florida. Bottleneck and Brahma Bull came up and we recorded the song *Hick Lyfe* and shot the video for it. After that, Bottleneck went back to Florida to pursue his solo career and Brahma Bull stayed at the farm to work with me. That's when Brahma Bull, Sneed, Orig, CB3, and I worked on the project called *Kinfoke.* It was similar to the *Kuntry Kitchen* project that had dropped almost a decade prior.

Jeff McCool, aka Brahma Bull: I'd never been in a studio, so it was cool. I called it the Kuntry Kitchen for about 3 days, because after that, I started calling it home. I literally lived there for close to a year. After we shot the *Hick Lyfe* video, I figured, "Hey, if this is going to happen, I've got to be around it!" So I asked Smo, "Hey man, what do you think about me staying here for a while?" We started booking shows and he was steady cranking out music and teaching me the ropes.

We booked some decent shows and were traveling a bit. My crew and I had a good reputation with promoters and owners because we were "easy to work with". We just tried to not make a mess and to clean up after ourselves if we did. Our typical rider back in those days included a half gallon of Jim Beam Red Stag, a case of Red Bull, and a case of Dr. Pepper. I don't drink anymore, but back when I did, I liked to make my two signature drinks. I called the Red Stag and Red Bull a Cock Fight and when I mixed the Stag with the Dr. Pepper, I called it a Backyard Boogie. Those were staples back in those days.

We were doing a show in Florida one night and I got a call from California. It was some guy saying he wanted to be my manager and I told him that I was not interested. At that time, we were doing everything on our own, and while I did need some help, I was getting a lot of offers from people and it was hard to keep up with who was who. I was sick of it by the time I heard from this guy and was just like beat it.

Dan: Smo had a couple million views on the *Kickin' It in Tennessee* video by the time I saw him. When you hear Smo rap, you know it's him because he's got his own tone and delivery. SMO is SMO, he's the first one, he's the last one, he's the only one. Until I'd heard Smo, I didn't take

Country Rap seriously, but as soon as I heard *Kickin' It in Tennessee*, I said, "Yep, I get it," and got in touch with him. Eventually, I was like, "Dude, we can do this!" I saw him as having the ability to make a statement for the whole genre, and thought if we knuckled down and worked hard, we could make this a real thing to take seriously because they're not going to have a choice.

So we left it like that, and it was another 5 or 6 months before we spoke again in May of 2011. In the meantime, I'd still been watching him online as his numbers continued to climb for *Kickin' It in Tennessee*. In the early spring of 2011, I got in touch with a woman named Madison who was working at a TV production company where there was interest in doing a reality show about Smo.

Little did I know, Dan was actually interested in me and continued to follow my music to see what I did. He said he wanted to come see a performance and I told him to come on. Sure enough, he showed up. It was in Tennessee at a small club, but the whole crowd was going crazy. I did the show and my usual meet and greet. After that, this guy came up to me and introduced himself as Dan Nelson and said he wanted to be my manager. He looked me right in the eye and told me what he could do for me and how we could accomplish our goals together.

> **Dan:** I flew out to a show in Tennessee at this redneck club. I looked very out of place but got settled by the side of the stage and watched the show. Afterward, I told him, "You killed it!"

A while after that, I had a show at a mud park in Texas. It was a big stage with like 4,000 people in the crowd. On top of that, Dan was there to watch me perform again. It was an awesome show and everybody had a great time. After my set, I went to the merch booth to sign autographs. Haystak taught me to only sign autographs until the next act starts. Once it's their turn, wait. It's respectful that way. I signed tons of autographs and then went back to kick it with my Kinfoke in the mud. That mud park performance became one of the first of many and the next day, we shot the mudding scenes for *Kuntry Boy Swag*.

> **Dan:** That night was hilarious. First of all, I'm from L.A. and had never been this deep into Texas, much less to a mud bog. I rented a truck and when I pulled up, I was escorted back to the stage and saw Smo and the guys getting ready for the show. I watched the live show and the crowd went NUTS! He stole that crowd, there was no doubt about it. He had people chanting his name!

The music was getting better but over time everyone decided to part ways and continue to work on their own projects. We had some great times back then and we have been lucky enough to continue to work with each other throughout the years. I was ready to take on a new project. After *American Made* came out, I wanted to work with Jon Conner more.

> **Jon:** Smo told me about this mud culture that was popping off big down south. I was happy to hear that the vision of mine had a home, that there was a culture building around it. I called him and said, "Look, I am just really intrigued by this whole culture, and this is a sound I want to explore further. You're the perfect voice to this sound and I think I can be a big help to what you're doing, I'd like to move down because imagine what we could do if we were together in the studio every day." Smo was all for it, "Man, come on down." So at the beginning of 2011, I jumped in the car with everything I could fit in it – including my wife – and we headed down to Tennessee to start working with Smo.

Orig the DJ: When we introduced Jon Conner with his *Kickin' It in Tennessee* sound, which was really his brainchild, I knew we were on to something big. In my opinion, Jon Conner was the very beginning of this sound.

We decided on a six song EP and I went to Delaware to work on it. By that time, we were doing lots of shows at mud parks and had gained tons of fans in the mud culture. We wrote *Kick Mud* and were so excited to have such a dope track to follow up *Kickin' It in Tennessee*. One of my other favorites on the EP is *Wanna Shuck*. It was awesome to work with local artist and good friend of mine, Jolie Bell on that song. For the artwork, Orig and I decided on a Mason jar with roots planted into the ground. It's one of my favorite designs. I named the EP *Grassroots* and released it independently.

Chapter 7:
Kuntry Livin'

Daddy served us proud
Red, white, and blue
And if he was here today,
He'd tell ya too
~ **Cause We Can**

Dan managed my first ever endorsement deal for one of the first e-cigarette companies called Safe Cig. Around that same time, the guys from Lizard Lick hit me up about doing their theme song. They were big fans of Hick Life, so we did a similar rendition called *Lick Life* and shot a video with the cast. Not too long after that, I got a call from an executive named Chris Stacey. At the time, he was head of Warner Nashville's Radio Department. Similar to John Rich, Chris was on the lake with his buddies when they stumbled across *Kickin' It in Tennessee* on YouTube and loved it! He commented, "Yo, this video is dope! I'm Chris Stacey from Warner Nashville." I responded back, "Yo, what's happening, this is Smo." He invited me to lunch and later listened to some of my music.

He believed I had real talent and was one of the first people in the industry to have my back. Later on when he was leaving Warner and I was trying to get signed, he still rooted for me and made it happen with Cris Lacey, head of A & R. I owe Chris Stacey (and Cris Lacey! Say those names together ten times fast!) tons of thanks for seeing my potential and I'm so thankful that he reached out to me that day! I told Dan about the meeting, so he contacted head of A & R, Cris Lacey. He told her to check my work out and that kicked off our relationship with Warner. All the excitement motivated me to work even harder on our new project *Kuntry Livin'*. It had been a decade since I had released *Kuntry Kitchen*. John Conner and Orig were the producers and we worked really well together. JC and Orig made an excellent team.

> **Jon:** We were out on the road every weekend. During the week we worked on music. Smo's manager told us Warner Nashville was interested in what we were doing and wanted to make sure our music was top notch. So that really lit a fire, to know people were paying attention and listening to what we were doing, to me it raised the stakes in the studio. Coming from an East Coast background, I had a certain idea and sound in mind which was super-hard drums and percussion with these dobroes and fiddles and banjos and just the juxtaposition of both of those to me was really cool.

> **Orig the DJ:** I loved looking at the reaction from the crowd when I would spin a new song. I also loved getting to hang out with the fans and just spending time with the ones you make the music for.

> **Jon:** We were doing everything ourselves, from videos to socials, the website, booking the live shows, everything was done by 5 or 6 guys. On the road, Smo let Alex King and me hold down the hypeman positions. It created this really cool dynamic on stage. I held down one side and Alex the

other. As a producer it was awesome to see the fans react to the music, then go back into the studio and say, "Oh if they liked that, they're gonna love this!"

Orig: When Smo finally got that opportunity with Warner, that's when Jon and I dove into the studio head first and spent literally 13 hours a day for a couple of years, really testing ourselves in so many ways. We're very self-motivated and overachievers, so by the time the big guys came into our lane, we had so much to offer.

JC and Alex were really into the visual side of the music. We had already done the video for *Kick Mud* together and it was doing so well that we decided to film a miniseries that we aired on YouTube at the same time every week. We called it *Kuntry Livin'*, which was also the name of the album. We were getting a lot of positive feedback on the music videos so we thought filming a "behind-the-scenes" approach about life on tour and the farm would be entertaining. It was the precursor to the reality show, and we got a lot of views and comments. I'm thankful to have those now because they're almost like a video diary during a great time in my career.

Jon: We shot more videos, created more buzz, released behind the scenes videos – most of which I shot – and gigging on the weekends, building the buzz louder and louder!

To this date, one of my favorite songs on that album is *Workin'*. It's one of my favorites to perform and it's definitely a #1 fan request. We were working our asses off and it just came to us that our Kinfoke needed an anthem to get us up and going to our jobs. I have had so many awesome experiences because of that song, like getting to do a lip sync video with the Murfreesboro Fire and Police Departments. Everyone has to work in some sort of way to get by and we wanted to provide the soundtrack for that. I never imagined it would be as big as it is today!

Relapse: I did some work-for-hire writing on *Workin'*, all four of us – Smo, Jon Conner, Alex King, and I – passed around a notebook for a couple hours and took turns writing lines, it was pretty cool. He made my lyrics sound real good.

I would have to say *Kuntry Livin'* was the most fun album to work on. Don't get me wrong, every album has been rewarding in its own way both educationally and just a good time! But back in the *Kuntry Livin'* days, we weren't starving artists anymore and we had just enough recognition that we were respected. The ball was still totally in our court and we were eager to have all those opportunities back then. It was a really cool time in my career. One of the most memorable writing sessions from that album was working on *Bumpy Road* with Rhett Akins and his son Thomas Rhett. This was before Thomas was who he is now, so to me I just looked at it as a father-son writing session. Now I look back and think of how cool it was that we didn't know what success was in store for me or Thomas Rhett just a few years down the road.

Rhett: I think I went out to Smo's farm two or three times to write, and Thomas Rhett went once, but the day Thomas Rhett and I went, we both loved it because it was one of those deals where anything goes. A lot of times, in any genre, you pretty much have to stick the script when you're writing a song, but with Big Smo, he didn't care what we wrote as long as we loved it and thought it was great. It was just a really great time to be with your son who loves rap music as much as you do and as much as Smo and those guys do, but they love Hank Jr. and Aerosmith, and we could just put all our ingredients that everybody had into one big pot, and make a song.

We were writing but we also played a game of Skeet Ball where I hit the golf balls with a driver, and they shot them with a shotgun.

> **Rhett:** That was a lot of fun! While Orig and Jon Conner were in there working on what we'd done, Smo, Thomas, and I went outside and invented this little game kind of like shooting skeet golf style, so Smo was driving golf balls off the tee and we'd shoot them with a shotgun. It was basically everything Smo does on a regular basis, but my wild side got to come out in everything on that trip, from shooting guns to writing whatever we felt like writing.

Everything was going really well, and we were still working really hard on *Kuntry Livin'*. We were in communication with Warner, but still trying to see what all was going to happen. It was an exciting time for us back then!

> **Shannon Houchins, CEO Average Joes Entertainment:** I went to the CMT Awards and was backstage. Peter Strickland from Warner Bros. was there, and Chris Stacey, and they grabbed me and said, "Hey, we need to talk to you. Have you ever heard of Big Smo?" I was like, "Yeah, he's great!" They said, "Well, we're thinking about signing him, and want to know what you think." I told them, "I think you guys should sign him!" So I encouraged them to do it. Average Joes had kind of become the authority on how to sell country rap, so they wanted to ask me. I told them, "Definitely do it!" So, I like to think I had a little bit of a hand in helping that happen.

We got the call that Warner wanted to talk, so we invited them to the farm. We wanted to show them what we were capable of in our own studio. We were doing well for ourselves on the road by now. We were booking some awesome gigs and had a lot of momentum with our first CMA Fest and BamaJam performances. These guys knew that we were working really hard, but we wanted them to see it with their own eyes. I was so proud to walk the executives into the studio right on the porch where we shot the artwork for *Kuntry Kitchen*. Hell, we basically lived in that studio for years, and it was awesome to finally have the chance to show off all our hard work to these people in the industry. It's what we had dreamed of since we were kids.

> **Orig the DJ:** We had Warner Bros Nashville's President and 20 Sony and APA executives all crammed in the Kuntry Kitchen. Just to have that moment was huge. So far nothing has trumped that yet. Smo would go to a meeting and would come back without CDs because everyone at the label wanted them for themselves. They seemed to really like what we were doing. My favorite reaction is always, "You guys made all of this music out of this little shack?!!"

> **Jon:** We met with the label when they came out to his farm in Unionville, including the President, John Esposito. We put on a performance and then we all headed into the stu-

dio. Dan turned the "meeting" over to me and it was my turn to show the Warner Bros. Records Nashville staff all the hard work we had done. We get about 3 records in, and Espo was dancing around the studio saying, 'We're gonna be rich!'

Everybody loved what we played, and that night was so surreal to me. It was a realization of a lot of childhood dreams, and we were all hyped up. The night ended and we were all reflecting around the bonfire and all I could say was, 'Wow!' The energy around that time was just amazing! We were doing killer shows, then coming home during the week to head back into the studio. It was just this pressure that I loved and fed off of, knowing the label was listening to everything we were making, and it just put this awesome vibe in the studio.

Dan: After that meeting out at Smo's farm, I remember sitting there with Smo and the heads of all the different departments. The last negotiating point I really left on the table was, "Look, if you guys are signing Smo to change him into something else, we will respectfully pass because we like who he is and what he's doing and think there's a future there," and Espo and the whole team said, "Nope, we get it and we love who he is. We just want to help make him a household name."

We got the offer a few days after that meeting, and I remember I called him SUPER excited from L.A. I told him, "Dude, you're going to be the first Country Rapper ever signed to a Major Label, EVER! Do you know what that means? You made history!"

Merch Dan found me at the airport

The most awesome experience during *Kuntry Livin'* was getting to write with so many different artists! Darius Rucker and I did *My Place* together which was absolutely surreal. I had been a Hootie fan for years. We were able to have a writing session on his tour bus and then he appeared on the TV show later. (Spoiler alert! Ha!) I met Casey Beathard back during the *Kuntry Livin'* days. I'm always amazed any time I get to work with Casey. Little did I know back then that we would write several hits together. Another writer I would like to credit is Bobby Pinson because together we wrote one of my all-time favorites *Redneck Rich*. I've been so fortunate to meet all the talented writers I have gotten to work with over the years.

Because I had signed a publishing deal with SonyATV, we got to record all the live instrumentation at Sony Studio A. This was my first time getting to work on my project in a really nice Nashville studio. All of our instruments before had been sampled, with the exception of a guitar or harmonica here and there, so this was also the first time I saw a full band play and record live. I told the guys the kind of vibe I wanted for *Lawdy Lawdy*. I said, "Think BTO's *Takin' Care of Business*." They were like, "Oh sure, easy!" So here was this guy JD on guitar, Rich Redmond who toured drumming for Jason Aldean, and Peter Keys the keyboardist for Lynyrd Skynyrd. They just started JAMMING and it was absolutely incredible. I remember being blown away. That's one of my favorite memories of recording *Kuntry Livin'*.

My last task to finish the album was to create the artwork for the album cover. Since the studio had been the launchpad for all of our dreams, I decided to pay homage to my Kuntry Kitchen cover and used the studio as my backdrop for *Kuntry Livin'*. I designed the artwork with Tony Delano aka EB Tight, who did the photography and graphics. I love that my old dog Jade is on the cover gnawing on a big ol' bone. She was so happy that day.

Kuntry Livin' was finally ready. After the months of recording, photo shoots, filming, writing, touring, and definitely not much sleeping, we sent everything off and waited. It was much like lighting the fuse on that bomb and waiting to see what happened to the Pepsi machine. I didn't know for sure what was going to happen, but I hoped it would BLOW UP! Well, sure enough, it did! *Kuntry Livin'* released on June 3, 2014 and within the next week Billboard Magazine said we were #9 on the Top 10 Country Music Album Charts and #3 on the rap charts.

I finally felt like everything was worth it. I remember when I had to have faith in this dream and pursue it full time. Looking back on the *Kuntry Livin'* days, I know that I made the right choice to believe in myself. I felt so accomplished with all of our hard work and we felt even better now that the world was paying attention.

Chapter 8:

Sharpie Stains

Aw lawdy lawdy
Look who came to party
We got everybody here tonight
All my fellas and my ladies
We gonna get a little crazy
On that whiskey, wine, beer, and shine.
~ Lawdy Lawdy

I've had some jobs that gave me callouses and blisters. These days, after hours of meeting and greeting, and signing autographs, it's not uncommon for me to be covered in Sharpie stains. But it's OK, it's a happy reminder of a job well done and lots of love from my Kinfoke. I never knew when we named my fan base that it would turn into what it has today.

Demun: Smo is a really down-to-earth individual. He's a genuine person and I feel like that has spoken louder than anything throughout his career. His generosity and his gratitude toward his fans was obvious years ago when I first started touring with him. After each of his shows, he would walk out there and stand and shake every person's hand that came to the show. Fans never forget that. I certainly didn't.

JJ: That's been his thing since the beginning, and still is. We're all just a bunch of regular, redneck, working class dudes from the country, and to us, these people come out and spend the money they worked hard for. It means a lot. He would stand and shake hands and sign autographs and take photos with literally every person in line. I think that's been and will remain a huge part of his success.

Bird Brooks, Moonshine Bandits: I think Smo is very in touch with his fans, and it's important to be able to do that. I think that's why he has been successful.

More and more people were listening to my music and I was starting to get more shows. By that time I had agreed to let Dan be my manager and we were working nonstop. *Grassroots* was really popular, and I was in shock that *Kickin' It in Tennessee* was still racking up millions of views on YouTube. Things were starting to gain momentum and we caught the attention of Frank Wing, one of the top guns at the Agency for Performing Arts. He was hip to what we were doing in the mud bog scene and liked my work. Not too long after that, I became one of the first country rap acts signed to a major booking agency.

Frank: You have to understand, Smo was an artist who was doing his thing off the beaten path. He didn't care about labels, and as a matter of fact, at first, he was kind of incredulous with me, like, "What? You think I can sign with a major label??" Still, I saw that it was a totally untapped market at that time, I didn't even know that genre existed! As soon as I drove out to his farm and met him, I knew immediately he was someone I wanted to work with. As I started doing more research, I confirmed that indeed this culture did exist, and it was not in the mainstream but was real and growing.

Even though I knew how to have a good time and do my job without making a scene, a lot of promoters and club owners were hesitant at first because it's a "rap show". But I always made sure to watch myself because the community around the shows back then was very tight-knit. I didn't know who knew what people, and I wanted to be invited back. I tried my best to establish a rapport with everyone.

> **Frank:** To Smo's credit, he worked his butt off. Man, in the early days, I saw him play some of the smallest roadhouses and night clubs you can imagine. It was crazy, and for two years, I booked him before he signed with Warner Bros.

I perform for a crowd of sixty like it's a crowd of six thousand! It turns out that the club owners where I performed let their buddies in the business know the kind of show I put on.

> **Frank:** Sure enough, more and more people started show- ing up. What really surprised me was when I went to visit some of these shows – whether in Ohio, Louisiana, wher- ever – people would show up. I started booking Smo in those kinds of markets right from the beginning. I saw the appeal across all ages. Kids would just show up at his shows. They really look up to Smo.

I mean, this guy is so accommodating with his fans, you wouldn't believe. It's near and dear to his heart, the stuff he does for his little Kinfoke. In my years working with him, he's never failed to fulfill a request from a fan. One particular favorite of mine, from back in August in 2015, was one that came in from a child that was terminal with Leukemia, and I had Smo give a personalized shout-out on video. Kids LOVE Smo, and he's always been a family-friendly brand and children just gravitate toward him. I'd never really seen that before.

I've gotten lots of really cool gifts from my fans over the years. If you've ever watched the TV show or been out to my farm, there are gnomes that were a gift from a fan strategically placed throughout the property. I get a lot of shirts, beard products, fishing gear, hunting stuff, and hot sauce. I also have a huge collection of fan art I've been given over the years. Once I was looking for a special kind of hat I'd worn at a Mud Bog in Texas and couldn't find one anywhere. I sent a picture to my dear fan Darcey Johnson and she crocheted a replica for me. It's that kind of love and loyalty that has always bonded me and my Kinfoke.

It sounds cliché to refer to my fans as family, but some of the people have been around for over twenty years. Kimmi and David bagged up individual CDs with hay (The Kuntry Boy Box Set) and helped me in so many ways over years. I'm thankful for their friendship and loyalty. I also want to give a shout out to my Texas Kinfoke because they are as loyal as loyal can get. They have been fans for a long time, and I appreciate all the years of love.

I also have been forever impacted by the fan experiences that have moved me. Sadly disease, illness, and loss are all realities we must face, and I have met some very courageous survivors in my life. I've also been called in to be with some people during their final day. On more than one occasion, my anticipated visit had come too late. One fan in particular I planned to meet as soon as I got home from being on the road, but she didn't make it through the night. It is powerful what music does to us as humans and for some of my fans, it got them through chemo or even helped them through their last days. I cannot help but being moved to tears by some of the stories. I was even inspired to write *The Message* based on a Facebook conversation with a young fan who had cancer. I'm thankful so many people have shared their heartaches and burdens, because let's face it, a hurt that's shared is way more bearable. From drug addiction recovery to suicide attempts, I've received the gamut of stories of fans' struggles and I just want everyone to know I understand. You gotta just keep your head up. Gotta keep your head up.

Veteran Duck Hunt with Sarge & the guys

Me with Murfreesboro Fire Department

Another group of Kinfoke I hold near and dear to my heart are my servicemen and women and our veterans. I always try to do whatever I can for them because they are the bravest group of people in our society. They are willing to serve for each and every one of us every day while sacrificing time away from the one's they love. I'm thankful that Matt Doak, a friend from my hometown, got to be on the EP artwork for *Bringin' It Home*. He's in a family FULL of civil servants and they give back to our community so much. He is the epitome of hero for our town and I wanted that to be captured as the visual for the music. It turned out amazing and I'm thankful he was willing to be a part of that. To my military, police, fire, rescue, emergency medical service kinfoke, thank you. I've been lucky enough to get to know many of you and I'm thankful for all you do.

Shout out to my Murfreesboro Fire and Police Department. I was contacted by my cousin Benji and his friend Ashley at MFD about a music project. She asked if I would be willing to allow them to use *Workin'* for a lip sync video and if any way possible, could I make an appearance. Hanging out rapping and cutting up with the whole fire and police departments in Murfreesboro was one of the coolest experiences of my career. I was so honored when they asked to use the song because it reminded me of the whole reason why we wrote it in the first place. This opportunity exceeded any expectation I could have imagined back then. Even more humbling, they awarded me with an honorary fireman plaque at the annual awards ceremony. I was even invited to do a cooking show that the fire department puts out on the Murfreesboro channel. It's my own healthy version of mom's famous "Quick Chick". So thank you to everyone involved with that project and all that came from it.

I've met a lot of kinfoke through the years. A while back I met a couple that told me about their child with autism. He struggled with communication, but with my music, he began to experience major breakthroughs. I was stunned and said I would love the chance to meet him. We agreed to meet at the visitor center in West Virginia where they give away the free peanuts. He was a great kid and I gave a him a Davy Crockett style coonskin cap. His dad gave me a super dope fishing hat with a Navy patch on it in honor of my dad. When I went inside the visitor center, a nice older lady at the register told me she recognized me from my t-shirt that was made for me by a fan. We talked for a while and I ended up adding her to the guest list.

She and her husband came out to the show that night! It's crazy that none of these Kinfoke knew each other or even know this all happened, but for me it's always so awesome to see how this family all weaves together.

Halloween is my favorite holiday even though I was born on Valentine's Day. I LOVE when I see pictures of my lil Kinfoke dressed as *ME* for Halloween. They are so cute and put in so much attention to detail, all the way down to the baldness and beard. It's flattering and I enjoy all the videos, pictures, and stories from my little fans. Social media has been a great way for me to meet new kinfoke. Speaking of socials, special thanks to Miss Pam Cook that checks all the messages on my socials. I could never maintain and manage all the communication without her help!

One particular fan turned family that I met via social media is Matt Julian. He's a Marine veteran with incredible talent in welding metals. He offered to make a fire pit for the Cumberland Caverns benefit and I was like, "Yeah, that would be awesome!" He's since made my mom a metal flower planter for her yard, several pieces for my house, my mic stand, and even a whole army's worth of weapons for the *Country Outlaw* music video. He's a great dude and I'm thankful for everything he has done.

Matt Julian can make anything you want

Me Alligator Hunting with Kuntry and Steve

Matt: It all started with the Big Smo fire pit. I remember whenever he threw me the idea, "Hey, can you make me a mic stand out of chains?!" and I did, and it looked really cool. Another of my favorites are the weapons I made for Smo's *Country Outlaw* video. I remember once I started sending him some pictures for some prototypes, he started sending me requests for his own designs and the producers of the video were sending in requests, so it became really collaborative. Smo wanted a double-headed fish fork with deer antlers, baseball bats with deer antlers and saw blades, I mean, there's chains welded together, lawn mower blades welded together, circular saw blades! I even made a sword from a giant two-man buck saw! I raided 3 of my neighbors' junk piles to make it all! Smo just likes to challenge me, where he'll send me a sketch of something and say, "Hey, make this!"

Colorado Bound

One guy I must definitely mention is my boy Danny Igo aka Kuntry. We met when I did a show in Florida a while back. It was like we had known each other for years, and this guy is hilarious. If you ever get to know Kuntry, your gut will hurt, and you'll get fat boy cramps laughing at him. I have had so many good times with him over the years and he's a brother to me.

> **Kuntry:** Smo was doing a show here in Florida at the Round Up. Me and my buddy were out one night, and he told me Smo was playing in town, so we rode over to check it out. At the end of the night, he was heading to his meet-and-greet and there was a long line of people, so I just walked past everybody, went right up to him, and said, "Big Smo, I'm Kuntry," and then he surprised me as I was walking away from the table and said, "Hey Kuntry, let's go hang out on the bus."
>
> I had a mason jar full of Moonshine with me at the time, and we just sat there the whole time talking while we were chilling, and I think we hit it off. That was the beginning of a relationship with a new best friend.

Kuntry ended up winning the Ultimate Kinfoke Experience on the Smo Mobile App. He came and stayed at my house for the weekend. It snowed and we went hunting with my best friend Steve, another fan turned fam. It's cool that now, Matt, Kuntry, and Steve are all friends.

Kuntry: It was dope when I got to be part of the Kinfoke Experience. He flew me to Nashville, picked me up himself from the airport, and we went to the Sony writer's house and he gave me a little tour and told me about the song-writers who come there to write and record. Then we went over to Warner Nashville and kind of did the tour, went around and met a few people, and of course, his pictures and videos were playing as we were walking through there and a bunch of other Warner Nashville artists. Then we went back to the farm, and he gave me a little tour of the Kuntry Kitchen studio out back, his grandfather's store, and showed me where it all started. We watched some movies, then went to Walmart to get some stuff for a hunting trip. He wanted hunting to be part of the Ultimate Kinfoke Experience. We went out in the woods one morning with his buddy Steve and froze our balls off in 5-degree weather. We got up the next day and he made deer omelets for breakfast. While I was there, he had me help him finish up a piece from his jewelry line, *Draped Jewelry*. From there, we went to Nashville to Alan Jackson's bar, and got a couple drinks, then went down and had some Sushi. I stayed right there on his farm and the whole weekend was an awesome experience.

Speaking of hunting with Steve and Kuntry, we have definitely had some good times together. For us, hunting is a way to get away from everything and have some peace and quiet. For me, it's good thinking time and a chance to clear my head. I eat what I kill and donate what I can't eat. Steve took me deer hunting for the first time and it was so awesome to get to experience that with my best friend. I'll never forget, he said, "Leave the guts. Coyotes gotta eat too." He's always wise like that. When Kuntry, Steve, and I go hunting, there's no telling what's going to happen. I will say it's a wonder we ever get any hunting done because we are always laughing so hard when we are together. Kuntry took Steve and me gator hunting and Steve killed the hog in the video for my new song *Bone Splitta*.

Steve is also way more experienced at hunting than I am, but he loves to share and teach me things. We have a great time when we go hunting together whether it's for deer or wild hogs. We went to Colorado together and I'm looking forward to our trip to Mexico on the Kinfoke Krewz. These guys were all fans that turned into brothers and I don't know what I would do without them. Needless to say, I have the best fans any artist could ask for. Some of these fans I have had since the very beginning and I'm thankful we have had this experience together.

Deer Stand Selfie

My parents always said
I had a cone head

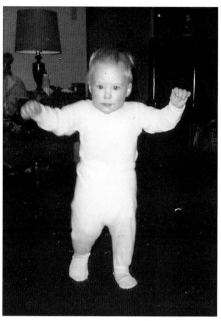

Movin On Up at an early age

Dad & Me

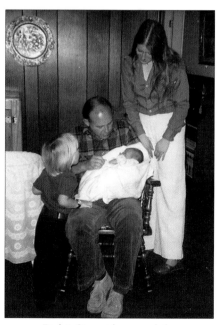

Dad & Sissy with me as a baby

#swagg

My mom, Chris and me as a baby

Exotic Dancer at 2.5 LOL

I stayed into shit

Momma Smo always had the best food

Momma Smo holding me as a baby

My mother couldn't keep up with me

1st side by side

It's a Party Over Here!

My Great Grandpa in front of the old store

Been a fan of the wagon since then

Look at This Kid Go!

All I want for Christmas...

Farming with my dad

I Love the old pictures of me & mom

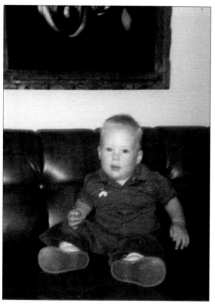
#likeaboss

Me and my sister

"Hi" "Da Da" I miss you. I Love you.

I am ordering pizza

I was into sports at a much younger age

Always On Clean Up

Mandy and me catching the bus

My first fish

I always loved goats

Dad with me, Chris and Sissy

Tonka WORKIN'

Rusty was my first dog

Chris and me, Chillin Like A Villian

Carl A Smith enlisted

Chris and me on vacay with Granny B

Me and Chris at Camp Boxwell

Looking a lot like Christmas

Scouts was my life

Me & Chris Pinewood Derby

What about that sweatshirt

WHY...

Grade School was always an awkward time
for me when it came to style

What a chunk I was

Walk Like an Egyptian

I always was a dog lover

WTF

Jeff & Phillip – Best Friends

Chris's Wedding Day

The King of Liberty School

Revisit California in the 7th Grade

Another Signature Shirt by my airbrush guy

Me with Mama & Granny B

Family Is Everything

THE MEN – Chris, Carl, & me

Family photo with Granny B

I love my parents

Chillin at the
River House

Whoa! Look at that cheese!

The Sweet Smith Family

Oh the days of braces

I need to stop with the teeth

A young me in the 80's

Box Cut with the $ chain...CLASSIC!

The Undercover Lover, my first car

G'ed Up

Pre Christmas Parade with the kids

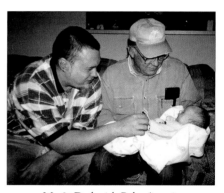

Me & Dad with Baby Ameria

Chris & Me Having Some Drinks

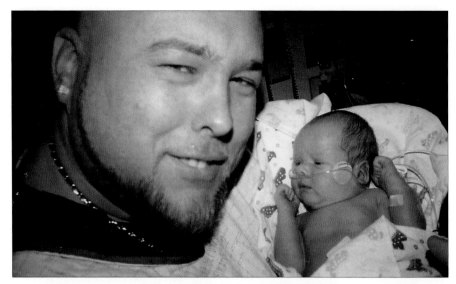
Welcome to the world Lanica Jade Smith

Me, Ameria & baby Lanica

Me and baby Lanica

Ameria Jammin' on the Drums

Me & Mom

Dad and Kelsey

This kid is too cute

My Kids are my life!

Me & my K5 Chevy

Me & Dad

My second low-rider station wagon

Cowboy Troy and Me

Me donating charity check on Fox 5

LIVE in YO Face

LOVE MY MOM

The LACs and me

Bubba Sparxxxx and me

Yelawolf and me

Tristan Jackson and his crew

Helping The Community

My Best Friend

Never been a Red Carpet Guy... till now!

Part III

AND SO IT IS WRITTEN

Chapter 9:

Talk of the Town

I got a heart of gold
With a backwood soul
A dream to own a lot more than I owe
A few heavy bills that's weighing me down
And I'm doin' what I can
Just to wait them out
~ **Redneck Rich**

When I was in the fourth or fifth grade at Liberty School, we went on a field trip to Nashville to sit in on a LIVE production of Talk of the Town on News Channel 5. I wore my dad's sports coat and combed my hair just in case the camera wound up on me. I didn't really know exactly what we were going to do that day at Talk of the Town, but I knew this could be my first big chance. When we got there, we each had to fill out these little information cards. Mine looked like this:

Name: John Smith
What's your dream in life: I want to be on TV.
What do you want to be when you grow up: I want to be on TV.
What's most important to you: I want to be seen on TV.

It worked! The lady called my name and said, "Well it says here that you want to be on TV! What would you like to say?" I grinned and said, "I wanna be seen."

> **Dan:** Our task was to ask, "Okay, how do we essentially get somebody else to pay millions of dollars to market this guy?" and TV was the fit because he's so good on camera. It was a branding dream come true because A&E later invested literally millions in promoting the show. Leading into the first season, for instance, they spent over a million dollars on marketing alone!
>
> Even though Warner came before the A&E deal, we were pursuing both at the same time, and actually had started out working with VH1 on a pilot for the idea. He was so natural and fantastic on camera. Smo's a character and he's very quick-witted and all of these things that you can't train somebody in, you either have it or you don't.

We had a lot of positive feedback from the *Kuntry Livin'* webisodes on YouTube and Dan was already talking about a TV show to several networks. We had been filming ourselves for years so everyone was natural on camera. We just captured our normal day-to-day routine, tour life, and pranking each other. We decided to take this TV show talk seriously and filmed our own sizzle reel. By this point, I had filmed an episode of Bar Rescue with Jon Taffer. He was a really awesome guy to work with! Thanks JT.

> **Dan:** As we went about doing this, we quickly learned that as good as we were with writing story lines, we were NOT sizzle reel editors, which is a very specialized talent. So we spoke with a guy named Dave Mace at A&E, and they were interested in what we were doing. After 3 days of try-

ing to get this edit right, we ended up sending him the original sizzle reel we had, and said straight up, "I know this is not great, we're not great at editing, but this is kind of what we're thinking."

The main point was to show them we knew what we were doing. Smo and I both wanted to have some creative control and a relationship with a network, not just a production company. We wanted to be able to say, "No, we're not going to do this, and if you challenge us, I'm just going to call the network." They had some production companies in mind they wanted to bring in. We landed with a company called Brownstone run by Drew Brown and Bob Gillan who were hungry, smart, and genuine, *and* A&E loved them.

JJ: It was a cool thing. At that point, we'd really pushed and pushed and pushed, documenting every part of our lives literally around the clock. By then, it was me, Alex King, Orig, Smo, and Jon Conner – just this tight-knit little group of workers we had, and we spent around-the-clock days out in that studio. There was always someone out there 24 hours a day, 7 days a week doing something to get it to the next level. I think it was Dan who told me they had a major network interested in possibly doing a reality show and had me go into the editing room to put together sizzle reels for an A, B, and C story, real short, like 3 minutes long. I remember sitting out there all night, jumping back and forth between Final Cut and Premier Pro, putting together these little highlight reels, and showed them to Smo and Dan the next morning. They liked them, so we sent them off.

Bob Gillan, A&E TV Show Producer: Brownstone Entertainment, my previous company, had a relationship with A&E. We'd done a show called Bar Rescue that was going on its third season, and we were trying to find other content to develop for A&E. Reality Shows kind of go in cycles, and at that time, Duck Dynasty was one of the shows that was popular for the network. The executive at A&E, Nicole Reed that we'd worked with on Barter Kings, spotted Big Smo and thought, "Wow, what a big, fun personality!" So we went and checked out some of the YouTube behind-the-scenes webisodes he'd been filming himself. We contacted his manager Dan about coming out to his farm in Unionville to shoot with him for a couple days to put our own sizzle reel presentation together for the Network.

Within that trip, we were also seeing who was in his life: his family, his friends, his band mates, and that is where we really got to know, and got a chance to see the backdrop of his farm. That cool little country store on the back of his property where he made music with his band members was awesome, and they were all pretty damn funny. After meeting everyone and seeing all that, our consensus within the production company was, "Wow, we've gotta jump on this NOW!" Initially, the show had a working title of "Big Country" which played on both BIG SMO and his country lifestyle. The biggest asset we had was John himself, who we quickly affirmed was a natural in front of the camera, very smart, and very good about knowing what his persona is and how he funnels it. His family was great, his mom and daughters were like undiscovered talent, so I thought, "Oh my God, this is great, his mom just tells it like it is and is really funny when they're together on screen." So we really liked the dynamic and the way everyone interacted with each other. When we were out there shooting for those first couple days, we all said, "You know what, he has that IT factor."

We filmed a six-month pilot for VH1, but they didn't seem to share our vision, so we did several months of filming with CMT. That also turned out to be different than what we intended. Luckily, things turned more of the direction we had aimed for when we were contacted by A&E. Dan and I wrote and filmed everything because we wanted to be in control of how we were shown to the whole world on TV. It was important to us to keep everything sincere and genuine.

> **Haden:** Alex King just always brought this crazy energy. I remember being NERVOUS! As we started filming, it was both terrifying and exciting at the same time, but I saw quickly that it was going to work. With his team, Smo, Dan and everyone involved, I knew it was going to go all the way!

Because being on your own TV show isn't something the average person gets to experience, let me tell you a little bit about it. First off, filming starts at around 6 am and goes until about 10 at night. This happens five, maybe six, days a week depending on the project's schedule. Before we began filming my show, I watched Jon Taffer come in and film his parts on Bar Rescue and then go about his business. I remember thinking, "That's it? I can't wait to do a TV show." Little did I realize, for a seasoned guy like himself, it is a lot easier.

We decided that the show would be filmed primarily at the farm. I live there with my family and that's where we do all the work on the music, so it seemed like the best place. I also thought it would help everyone feel at ease if we filmed at a familiar location. It's our home. It's a reality show. It seemed totally logical. What I had not foreseen was having a crew of at least 20 people at my house nonstop. They had a trailer in the hay field that was their office. They were an excellent crew and I cannot thank them enough for all of their hard work, but they know as well as I do, we had some rough days.

> **Dan:** Smo has a natural talent as a writer and we wanted to retain a certain amount of narrative authority. Smo would handle a lot of the family content, and I would handle the business stuff. The great thing with Smo is, he was not afraid to put in the work when he knows the end result is going to be a great product.

> **Bob:** In reality TV, there's a Hot Sheet where someone takes notes all day on set. Then they compress that into a one- or two-page summary email that basically says, "Here are all the interesting things that happened today." Sometimes we'd insert little bits of dialogue that were really funny. One thing about a reality show is you don't want to try and create story lines yourself; you want to observe as much as possible. Even though this is kind of a sitcom-reality show type show, we would ask Smo in advance, "Well, what do you normally do?" Then what we'd do is, ahead of each season, we talked at length with Smo and Dan and ask, "What's coming up with the band, family, etc.?" That gave us a sense of their calendar, and from there, we'd develop an outline of scenarios and topics, and all figured out together which ones worked really well for an episode.

The other big thing was we wanted Smo and his family to feel relaxed in their own environment, and that's what was important about shooting principally on the farm. It was the ultimate farm. You have cows in the distance, a barn, acres of land, and it personified in a small little world what this part of Tennessee was. What I loved most that behind his house sat this little country store. It ended up being the perfect backdrop – even with Tennessee in winter! There was a lot we were trying to get shot in one day, and we were shooting outside, so we were always up against a time pressure and hampered by the amount of sunlight for the day. It was always a very tight schedule and we needed to make sure everybody was up and able to shoot starting early in the morning.

We tried to capture them all in their routines as much as possible too to make everyone more comfortable in scenes on screen. Whatever felt most natural to the whole cast. We tried to accomplish that in episodic ways. That kept things focused. The other thing was that everyone was new to this, so we had to make sure we kept them all happy because we needed their cooperation with the tight shooting schedule. Smo as a Producing Partner always had his eye on the bigger picture.

JJ: The first couple weeks of shooting, there was some stumbling over lines but for the most part it was an unscripted show. Obviously, they couldn't be able to just put cameras on us and film everything we do because they wouldn't have been able to put together a story line, so what they would do was suggest scenarios, or put us in scenarios and film what actually happened. I know a lot of people feel like that show was completely scripted, and I can see how it feels that way because even though it wasn't, we'd have to go back and re-shoot scenes at different angles or close-ups, so we might have to repeat the same scene 4 or 5 different times constantly for everything we did. So at a certain point when you're saying the same line for the 5th time, it started to seem like we were scripting things.

It was a challenge for me to get into groove with it for sure, because never having any acting experience or any kind of camera experience other than being behind one. Most of the time, in my life I was the one filming stuff, so being in front of the camera was definitely a different thing for me. But once we got the hang of it, it wasn't too bad, and we needed a goof ball character – someone who wasn't so serious all the time about everything – and that's kind of where I fit in. Me being a utility guy, who edited and tour managed and ran merch and did some of Smo's day-to-day managing, booked his family vacations and planned his family trips, everything in his life, and because I was driving the bus, they decided for the show it was best to make my character the bus driver. So I became kind of the goof ball in the group, the comic relief, along with Smo of course!

Obviously, none of us are trained actors so it had its frustrations, but no one was as surprising on camera as the one and only Momma Smo.

Lanica: She loves everything about being Momma Smo! She gets a kick out of it. It was so funny, there was this one episode where she was cooking and they were filming it, and she whipped out the wooden spoon!

Ameria: We watched the commercial and all of us were dying laughing. She was crying she thought it was so funny. They were making a YouTube video with my dad filming Nanny cooking and she looked at the camera and said, "Hello, this is Momma Smo in the kitchen with her wooden spoon!" With the cookbook, I was there when we were doing the photo shoot and everything, it took forever!

Bob: That was the surprise one, because when we met Mary Jane, everyone was like, "Oh my God she's FUNNY!" Because she tells it like it is. I liked their dynamic and they definitely had a rapport. That's why both the network and us after seeing some early footage of them together all agreed, "Okay, we've got to figure out as many mom and Smo scenes, whatever they are," and that was really fun and was real. At the same time, we always tried to be very respectful because we were shooting in her home and didn't want to exhaust her. We wanted to shoot and get out of there.

Dan: I can't speak highly enough about Mary Jane. She's so sweet and so natural and funny on camera. I looked forward to shooting scenes with her just because it was very easy. She owned the scenes she was in and, honestly, some of my favorite scenes from both seasons involved his mother. Smo has his mother's sense of humor.

Bob: As we went into shooting, it was about him as a father and son because his kids and mother were part of the show. So it was about focusing on how we bring out funny, interesting scenes and dialogue with him and his family.

Along with my mom, shooting with the girls was an awesome experience. They were so excited when we first found out about the possibility. We decided to write them in based on things that were important in their lives like Lanica going to a dance with her friends and Ameria learning to drive. My favorite part of filming with my girls was all the time we got to spend together. I was on the road a lot when they were young, so it was nice to get to have them with me while I worked. It was also cool to get to share a job with my kids because we all better understood each other's frustration because we were all living the TV show. I'm thankful that I have those memories with my daughters.

Bob: We always loved shooting scenes between Smo and his daughters too. One of my favorites was the episode where they bring home a pet piglet and Smo's reaction was basically, "Oh God, another pet!" I think what I liked best about them is he would have fun with them, and they would have fun with him. Because musicians are on the road a lot, what I saw that the girls liked most about working with their Dad on the show was the chance to spend time with him. They loved the fact that the show became a way to have that extra time with their Dad, and that they had that chance to bond – even if it was in front of the camera. Smo was understandably very protective of his daughters and I think they got comfortable around us and trusted us when we were shooting with them

Ameria: My favorite episodes from the show were when we got to do a bowling episode, and we got to go to a mudbog, and we drove down in a cool motor home.

Lanica: I had to make a 4-H project, so I decided to make a recycled trash monster. My dad and I were trying to get a cereal box and bottles and stuff, and we went in the production crew trailer and asked them to help. It turned out to be a really good project too and this wasn't filmed. We had one episode we filmed in the second season where I went to a school dance and was with my friends and we had a lot of fun.

Ameria: Everybody loves when he blended our cereal and makes us breakfast milkshakes, but it's not what we really eat for breakfast!

Lanica: I think we were on our way to town driving the first time my dad was talking about it to us and I was just like, "A TV show?", but I got used to having the cameras around.

Ameria: I got used to it too. It didn't really matter, I said I'd do it, it could be cool. It was fun. Whenever we were on camera, they gave us an idea of what to do and we'd make up everything. I really liked the production crew; they were really cool. Whenever we did interviews, they'd make sure we had a little snack after school. I just got used to it. It was something that was going on in our lives. When we got the store, I started working there.

Lanica: We're ourselves in our own way on screen, and then just seeing that character on TV I looked at it as a character after a while.

Ameria: The only thing I didn't like was I missed a lot of school because of doing the TV show. That was the deal breaker for me!

Aside from my family, I enjoyed shooting scenes with the band, especially when there was a cameo and we got the chance to hang with a guest artist. My all-time favorite performance the band and I did on the show was when we opened for Lynyrd Skynyrd! That was a dream come true for me. I got to freestyle a verse on *Sweet Home Alabama* in front of thousands of people! Now here's a good opportunity for me to share if you haven't already caught it. Remember I said I wrote *My Place* with Darius Rucker on his tour bus, well if you watch the show, we filmed my band "writing" *My Place* while "camping together". Sorry folks, that was fake, but drinking from the creek with John Rich was ALL TOO REAL and I had the stomach infection to prove it!

Another episode that stands out to me is when I bought my tour bus. Now I have traveled all over the country (and even parts of the world) in some sketchy buses. I have even taken a four-hour Maya mountain ride through Belize in an old American school bus (thanks, SB). But I can tell you that the little time traveling in the Swag Wagon was both the best and the worst of times. I was so happy when I got to "bury" the Swag Wagon on the TV show and get my very own tour bus.

Haden: We felt like kings when we got that tour bus, like we'd made it because it was very nice. We started touring in the Swag Wagon, which was a leaky old church van, and when we first started, there were just seats in there and you had to try and lay down any way you could, sleeping in these messed-up positions. Then you had water leaking on your head if it was raining, and there was no way you're getting good sleep. It was horrible but we made it work, and in the summer, when we played Texas in that thing it would be so hot, so you'd just be in that bus sweating bullets with no refuge. Eventually, they ripped out the seats and put in these leather couches that laid down into beds and even with those things, if you hit a bump in the road, they would launch you FIVE FEET in the air! I literally remember the bass player and I sleeping where we'd wake up in mid-bump just looking at the terror in each other's eyes and then falling back down, it was just crazy shit!

Demun: At the time I was doing some solo work and had done some shows with Smo. He was always a great guy and made sure that I was taken care of. Smo saw that I was traveling in a van with my band, so he gave me the Swag Wagon to tour in! He mailed me the title and said it's yours. I have lots of love for Smo.

We filmed on the bus when we were on the road and at the farm when we weren't. By this time I had a relationship with a guy named Captain Rodney that makes my Meat Mud. If you don't know about Meat Mud, let me let my buddy Andy explain.

Andy: That's my grandmother's recipe. She used to slow-cook a Pork loin in the oven for 8 hours and would mop it with apple cider vinegar and brown sugar. At the end of that, she'd take all the drippings and apple cider vinegar and brown sugar and add molasses and ketch-up and make a BBQ Sauce. Well, Smo and I both had a buddy who'd opened up a BBQ restaurant in Shelbyville called Uncle Sonny's. He'd had my grandmother's BBQ sauce before and asked me to make it for him and I made it. His restaurant got busier and busier and I was making probably 10 5-gallon buckets a week for him. It got really crazy!

Smo's always been a huge fan of it, so back when he was doing all these shows in these local spots, he said "Man, we should sell this BBQ sauce with my T-shirts and call it Meat Mud." I said, "Hell yeah!" Next thing I knew, we started making it and putting it in these mason jars, and he got a nice label made. In the beginning, I would go to some of the shows with him and sell merchandise, and we put that BBQ sauce out there and it got a little following too.

He'd mention it in his songs, and Smo bought the rights to it from me. Now somebody else makes and manufactures it. It's awesome to me that it grew into that!

Thanks, Andy! Now that somebody else that's making and manufacturing the sauce is Captain Rodney. He owned a store front in Bell Buckle at the time, and I thought it would be great for filming and selling my merchandise.

Dan: He texted me a picture of a key and said, "We have a store!" Immediately, I just freaked out! My first reaction was, "What are you gonna sell? What does it cost? Who are you hiring?" I was thinking, "Great idea in theory," but could see he was excited about it so I said, "Cool man, well why don't you come over and we'll talk about it and come up with a plan!"

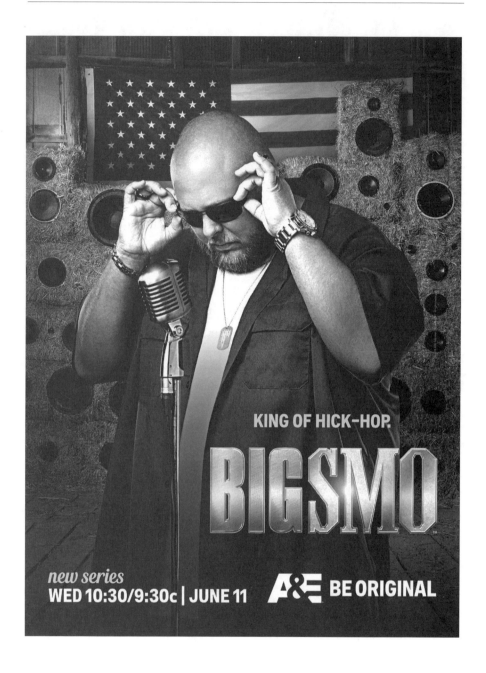

At the time, we were developing an entire line of products for the Big Smo brand: Meat Mud, Sweet Tea Sauce, Kuntry Caramel, Peach Pie Jelly, Apple Pie Jelly, Tomato Gravy, Kuntry Gravy, and the Muddy Mary Mix. We decided the new store was the perfect place to sell all these items! We did a major renovation and some decorating, and the store was ready. We filmed the grand opening of the store on the show and the mayor presented me with a key to the town. We finally had a place to go where we could film and have people come for signings. The TV show was great, but people had started to show up at my home to see me. I understand I lived my life on TV, but I never expected people would come to see me there. The store was a great place for me to see fans, film the show, and have a place to showcase my merchandise. It was also Ameria's first job! She did everything from ordering inventory to balancing the register every day. She ran the store and I'm so thankful that it was around for that.

Looking back on the TV show, what made me the most nervous is that we did all the work and all the filming and aired it to millions of people. This was the first time something that was filmed of me and was going out to a mass group of people and I didn't have the control I was used to. We were filming Season 2 while Season 1 was premiering, so we paused from Season 2 to watch Season 1 together. It was crazy!

> **JJ:** When they first sent us a preview before it was scheduled to debut on live TV, it was like a week before the first episode aired, it was kind of crazy seeing ourselves on TV and being there, even now going back and watching it, it's like, "Yo, we really did that," and "it's not something a lot of people get to do."
>
> **Ameria:** It was crazy, we were all here when we saw it on TV first, and it was like, "What!??" The music and every-

thing, it was cool. I didn't think it would ever happen, but it did.

Lanica: It was fun, because when we first saw it, it was super-cool, like, "This is actually happening!"

Dan: We went to New York City, and there was Smo's face and the name of the show on the sides of buses rolling around through Times Square and all over Manhattan. Then there were billboards all over the country, on the side of highways in the country and driving down the Sunset Strip in Los Angeles. I give all the credit in the world to both the branding and marketing teams at A&E and Warner Bros. because they worked hand-in-hand to make it all happen.

Bird Brooks, Moonshine Bandits: He'd been grinding for a long time, and it's been awesome to watch his success, and all the wonderful things that have happened to him, especially the TV show.

By the end of Season 1, I realized I was made for camera, but maybe I had over committed. I shared so much on Season 1, that by the time Season 2 came, I felt like maybe I needed to get back to music. I shared the work, the play, the on time, the off time, did the tricks for the camera and all. I was built for performing on camera, but I'm done with my personal life on screen. Thank you for the opportunity to share our lives with you, but (almost five years later now) there *won't* be a season 3.

Chapter 10:

The Resurrection

Friends from then are like family now
Where we used to kick it
Is where we still throw down
Some moved off but they came back around and it's all good
~ I'm Still Here

By 2015 so much was going on both professionally and personally. We had the show, the new Warner deal, my mom's health scare, my oldest daughter starting to drive, and my lifestyle choices weren't the best at the time. We had just finished filming Season 2 and I was headed out to the West Coast to start a month-long tour. I noticed for a few weeks that I had a horrible pain in my shoulder, and I figured I had pulled something. By this point I was in the worst shape of my life at 39 but was still jumping around doing 90-minute performances several nights a week. Looking back that little bit of exercise may have been what had saved me all these years. I wasn't taking care of my body and my eating habits had hit an all-time extreme. I love food. I love to have a good time and unfortunately a lot of the things I was choosing to overindulge in were literally killing me. That combined with everything going on with the TV show *and* the music, I was stressed. It was a very exciting time and a very busy time, but all the while I had this nagging shoulder pain.

We headed out to California and by that time the shoulder pain was more like a gorilla standing on my chest. At first it came and went a few seconds at a time, but eventually I got to where I couldn't walk ten feet without having to sit down. One night in San Diego, I had just finished a performance and couldn't sleep, so I was trying to get from the hotel to the bus. I definitely was not at a good point in my life. I was unhappy even though I had it all. Let me tell you, more money more problems is real.

I had the most people relying on me to get paid and to be provided for than I had ever had in my lifetime. The TV show had been an even bigger hit than I had imagined, and I was so busy that I was exhausted. I was dealing with too much at home and things had gotten to a point that I just didn't even care if my heart did explode right there in that lobby. It was already broken anyway. So I trudged through the lobby and collapsed onto a sofa in the city where I was born. I even laughed to myself when I thought about how it would sound-he had it all, a TV show, a West Coast tour, a beautiful family, and he dropped dead in a hotel lobby in his birth town. That's literally the last thing I thought before I was shaken back to life by my buddy Mike.

> **Mike Lowrey, Personal Assistant/Security/Bus Driver:** If Smo tells anybody about me, he tells them I'm one that actually saved his life. I started my career in the entertainment industry being a driver for different celebrities. I moved from Baltimore to Atlanta in 1995, and then in 2009, after working different transportation jobs, I decided one day I was going to start my own company driving celebrities. That led to several years where I drove tour buses with different celebrities including Young Thug on his

first tour, August Alsina, T.I., Future, Tyler Perry, in 2018 I started off with K. Michelle to Kendrick Lamar, and then from Kendrick to Jay Z and Beyoncé and then wrapped up last year with the Lil Wayne tour.

I first met Smo in 2013, and the tour bus I was partnered with in Atlanta, called me and said, "Hey, we've got a partner that lives in Tennessee, and we need you to drive him for 2 weeks." So, they sent me the paperwork and we had a midnight pickup. Now, I'm not one of those types of drivers who looks at someone's name on paperwork and then Googles and researches who it is ahead of time. So all I did was make sure I was there at the midnight pickup time, and I remember pulling this tour bus in the middle of the country, which is not normally where we do pick-ups at! It was dark out, so all I saw was open fields, and when I turned in the gate, he directed me to drive around the backside of his house. Once I did, he came out to greet everybody and he instantly told me how great he felt about us heading out on our journey because I didn't run over any of his bricks in his little circle. Drivers who had come up there had run those bricks over previously a bunch of times.

My policy is as long as all eyes are intact and the bus is still in an upright position, everything else is all good. So over those 2 weeks on tour, he was his normal, Smo self, all smoking, all drinking, the original Big Smo, 300+ pounds, super-lovable guy. Before we'd get to the venue, he'd come up to the front of the bus and we'd get to chit-chatting. It would be like 10 in the morning, and he didn't have anything to do right away. So we got into a routine where, as the band started unloading the trailer, because his hotel room usually wouldn't be ready to check into until later in the early afternoon, he'd usually ask me if I wouldn't mind walking around the neighborhood with him. So we'd do that every day, and it was during that time that we first realized we had this natural brotherly chemistry and love for each other. Whenever we encountered his fans or people who would recognize him in public, he always had a genuine love for them as fans and family. So I started really loving the guy when I saw how every time we'd walk somewhere, if someone recognized him, he would instantly treat them like they were true Kinfoke.

Once that two-week tour wrapped up and I got the bus back to the farm, he came around to the front while everybody was unloading, and said, "Man, I've got to talk to my management to see how I can afford to keep you around me all the time." To be honest, at that time, I'd heard so many artists say that, but nobody ever cut a check, that at first, I didn't put a lot of stock in it, and said, "Yeah, okay, cool" and pulled off and that was it. But sure enough, about a week later, management called and explained they were going to be going out on a tour for a month and a half and Smo wanted me to go out with him on the road. The problem was, they didn't have a job for me because they'd gotten a bus from another company that came with a driver as a package deal of some kind. So what I suggested to Smo and his team was that I act as his personal assistant and security, because up to that point, he didn't have a designated security guy or personal assistant during those two weeks I'd been out with him.

One day on the tour we got off the bus and were about to walk to Walmart and I'll never forget it, we literally took 3 steps away from the bus and he stopped and had this puzzled look on his face. I still remember looking at him and asking, "What's up?", and he said he felt like he had a gorilla pressing its thumb to his chest pushing it all the way to his back! His eyes looked like he was ready to cry, so I could tell something wasn't right, because throughout the day, as we would take a few steps any time he walked, he said he felt that same pressure. At that point, I started communicating with Dan and his assistant back in Tennessee, texting them all saying, "Something ain't right, this man is looking me in my eyes, complaining about having chest pains. We need to get him checked out ASAP."

Their response at first was, "He needs to stop smoking, he needs to stop stressing," and I replied, "Yeah, he probably needs to do all those things, but something is not right."

Up until the San Diego show, I relied on Tiger Balm and handfuls of baby aspirins to get by. I went to several different doctors and was diagnosed with low potassium, anxiety, and stress. I had taken medical stress tests and everything to find out what my issue was! I got into sucking on oxygen tanks because it kept me going. Mike Lowrey and Dan helped me get a grip on my eating habits. I just so happened to have a show in Minnesota. I was already aware that the Mayo Clinic was there because I had gone there years earlier when my skin got to its worst. I was in my early twenties and I was so miserable a doctor referred me there. I was quarantined for almost two weeks and given weird tar baths by nurses in hazmat suits. It was bizarre but it worked, so I knew I needed to get back to the Mayo Clinic and get fixed.

Mike: It's true! We were in San Diego and we were getting ready to leave and head to the next state, and he couldn't make it out of the lobby. We were literally about to rush him to the emergency room right there when we found him passed out in a chair in the lobby, and he told me, "I can't do it, I can't move." I asked if he needed us to call

9-11? Smo being the man he is, sucked it up and said, "Alright, let's get on the bus and go." In my mind, I knew something was not right, and kept communicating that to management, and decided on my own to change his eating habits. That meant getting him an entire month's worth of food from Fit Foods, where all of the calories from each meal were already on the box. He told me to feel free to take control of that. So every morning when he woke up, I got out of my bunk and he'd be in the front lounge and I'd make him breakfast and give him his options. Then I'd prepare it for him, and the same routine for lunch and dinner.

At the first appointment, the doctor asked about my lifestyle choices. I cannot deny to any of you the amount of alcohol I consumed at the time. If you knew me around that time, it was standard to start the performance with me chugging a quarter bottle of a fifth of Red Stag. That was how I started every show, followed with who knows how many gallons of soda over the years with it. It's horrible to think about now. I'm all for having a good time but looking back that wasn't a good time.

I was consuming entirely too much alcohol. The doctors said I had to quit everything — the drinking, the smoking, the bad eating. They did tests, blood work, and an ultrasound. Finally, I got the news from the doctor that I had 4 blocked arteries — three were 75% blocked and one was 100% blocked. I urgently needed open heart surgery. I found a doctor that I really liked. He said he did over 200 successful heart surgeries a year and his name was John, too. I went back to a hotel room and spent the next seven days getting my affairs in order for a quadruple heart bypass at 39.

That week of total sobriety brought clarity to so many things in my life from my relationships to my profession. I spent the week calling the people I love and preparing my kids for something they were having to deal with from over 800 miles away. All the while, we were trying so hard to keep as much away from the media as possible. The doctors told me that my new lifestyle had to become my new habits, essentially making a new me. I was adjusting to healthy eating and reasonable sized portions by the time of my surgery and the week of not partying had me feeling really good. On the morning of the heart surgery, I went in prepared to go out for good but so hopeful to get to wake up to a brand new me.

> **Chris:** As he was being wheeled into surgery, we were singing back and forth *Don't Believe Me Just Watch* by Bruno Mars.

Apparently, I fell asleep before the surgery even started. By this point, I was so ready to either be out of pain or feeling better, I almost didn't care about the outcome of the surgery. My love for my daughters really got me through that time because everything else was just not what I had hoped for in my life. I was under the most stress I had ever been, and I was definitely at a very low place emotionally. I was ready for an end or a change, or at least as ready as I could have ever been.

If you're squeamish, don't read this paragraph. For my quadruple heart bypass, they cut me from the base of my neck thirteen inches down the middle of my chest. They then sawed the breastbone apart and propped it open while they took two arteries from the backside of my breastplate and replaced the worst ones in my heart. Then, they basically reconstructed all the damaged parts, wired the breastbone back together, and glued me shut.

OK, you can come back squeamish readers. I remember seeing a clock on the wall when I came to and thinking that if the second hand is moving, I'm alive. It was the longest second of my life. I watched the red hand tick around the whole circle and thought to myself, "This is the first minute of my second chance at life." My first word was, "Water."

I had tubes and cables and tape and wires, the whole nine yards. Apparently, I threw a little temper tantrum (imagine that) but I don't remember. After a few hours of recovery, I walked the whole length of the hallway without even having to stop to catch my breath. I was a new man!

> **Chris:** During recovery, I remember I was kind of his coach, trying to get him up and out of bed, watching his breathing, keeping everything going to keep him going and keep his mind right.

I had an incredible staff of doctors and nurses and the most excellent care at the Mayo Clinic. I cannot thank them enough for saving my life. Dr. John, you're the man! To my staff of nurses, y'all rock. Thank you so much!

After they yanked out the tubes in my chest (yes, yanked them out), I was on my way to recovery. It is still crazy to me when I think back on it, that moment in recovery I already knew I felt better. That's how bad off I had been before. It was finally time to go home, so Dan got me a super fancy tour bus with huge leather recliners for the 12-hour ride home from Minnesota. I had already decided before the surgery A LOT of things were about to change, and on that ride home I dreamed about my new life.

> **Chris:** During that same time, Dan and I were making sure everything was prepared for him when he got home. That meant making sure there was a hospital bed there for him at his house, and when he went through the surgery, there

was sobriety that had also happened. As a consequence, his head started to clear, and not only that, to be real, that was going to put a serious hindrance on his ability to perform and be an entertainer for a while. It was going to have an impact on his ability to make a living, and I knew what that meant to him. Once he got home with a clear head and started to learn that things weren't being managed correctly and his relationships weren't what they could be, he started pushing people away that weren't in his best interest. It was his moment of clarity.

It's funny how changing your lifestyle makes people act differently. I wasn't partying anymore, so I didn't have quite the gathering of people around me like I was used to. The farm was a ghost town. During my recovery I changed my entire way of eating. I only eat red meat on *rare* occasions, and I never eat pork. I try to maintain a whole foods approach and think most things are OK in moderation. As a result, I lost over 100 pounds. Without a doubt eliminating alcohol was the best thing I have ever done for my health. I had such a clearer head and was so much happier without alcohol in my life. Even now, I don't drink it at all.

I have to spend a lot of time around drunk people when I perform and it's sad to see how habitual overconsumption of alcohol just really ruins people. I'm totally down for anyone to have a good time and enjoy themselves, but if you are drinking too much, I encourage you to assess your habits and make a change. It's the best thing I've ever done. Aside from the healthy eating and the sobriety, removing toxic relationships was the next thing I had to do to recover. From friendships to professional relationships, some people had to go for me to be able to survive my own life. My emotions and my bank account were being sucked dry by more than one person, and I had to do what was best for me and my kids.

Don't get me wrong, I tried everything I could to save at least one of those relationships, but change in a partnership is really hard, especially if only one side is ready and willing. The year after my heart surgery was one of the best and worst years of my life at the same time. So many things had finally been made evident and because I had a second chance at life, I was ready to live it to the fullest. I'm thankful to Dan, Chris, and my girls for helping me get through that year of recovery. So many others also helped through that time and I'm thankful for those that stuck around and kept progress moving. A few weeks after recovering from the surgery, I moved in with Dan because being at the farm had become too stressful and I needed to be in a space where my recovery could be my priority.

> **Steve:** Since he's had that heart surgery, it's been a 360 turn. It's been a world of difference.

> **Ladybug:** We thought we were going to lose a good friend, a good man, very scary...

> **JJ:** When he went through his heart surgery, at that point, we were really pushing hard, out on the road for two months at a time, and it strained on his relationships really hard. After he came home from the surgery and really started to get healthy, it weeded out fast who had really just been there to party.

> **Chris:** He realized some people weren't around for the right reasons. It was a realization he had to come to on his own. In some cases, not even I could tell him that. He had to see it for himself and he went through a transition and a lifestyle change, which meant the circle of people around him changed. He was going to be living a different lifestyle, and I was there – not every day – but certainly there during

moments of crazy times to support him during that transition. He has a pretty good group of folks around him now that I've learned to trust.

Andy: That was an upsetting time for me, I thought there for a second, I was gonna lose my best friend. We can go a year without laying eyes on each other, and then the next time we see each other, it's like it was just yesterday. If you ever find somebody you can get along with like that, that's a friend. He was there when my first son was born, he was best man at my wedding, and has been with me through everything important in my life. When he called me up and told me, I cried, I got upset. I called every day to check in and was so happy to see him come out the back end of that. He looks better than he's ever looked, and it's been a hard road and to see him turn it around is awesome because I know he'll be sticking around. That's all I care about, because without him, my life would be too sad to think about.

Mike: He was totally alone, because think about it, for an undetermined period of time, he wasn't going out on tour and interacting with all the fans or make a living. He wasn't able to go into the studio and make music, and he had no idea when his life was going to return to normal.

The surgery had canceled my tour for months, and with the medical expenses and now a huge business loss, I had to get very serious about my budget and start making some money. At that time *Bringin' It Home* dropped and Season 2 was about to air. People don't realize how much time passes between a show being filmed and aired, so in reality a whole year had passed. I had heart surgery between the time that was filmed and premiered, and by that point, *so much* in my life had changed. I decided to make *a lot* of personal and professional decisions to try to find happiness and rein in some of the extravagant business expenses. That even included closing the doors on Big Smo's Kuntry Store. We decided that the show had run its course for us, and Dan and I set out to start rebuilding Big Smo Inc. I dove back into the studio hard, a new man ready to make some new music.

A serious side note to my kinfoke and readers, listen to your body when it's sending you signals that something isn't right. What I thought was shoulder pain could have become a massive heart attack at any moment. Love your body and take care of it with healthy foods and fun in moderation. Get some exercise and let lots of healthy good love and people in your life. You only get one.

Chapter 11:

The Exodus

I used to think that I was stuck
But then I changed my luck
I'm movin' on up

~ **Movin' On Up**

While I was recovering, I was able to get some thinking and writing done. Little by little I was getting better and better. I walked miles a day and was the most active I had been in my life up to that point. I was feeling great. The first time back in the studio I was nervous. When you have heart surgery every single movement hurts for a while. Your chest is required for so many things, coughing, sneezing, breathing, *everything*. I'll never forget the very first time back in the vocal booth it HURT so bad. Thankfully, my producer Jason Mater worked with me and helped me ease back in. Rapping requires a lot of breathing and pushing sound out, and I had to retrain my body on how to create my tone. It didn't take long though and I realized with a new heart, *I was on fire!*

> **Jason:** When we went in the studio that first day, Smo could barely keep his breath. Producing that session was mainly about trying to keep him engaged knowing he

was going through a lot of pain recovering and couldn't lay down vocals. He just wasn't going to. We tried it for one day, but his vocal tone is naturally taxing on the vocal cords. Interestingly enough, our vocal cords were never meant to make sound. Humans decided to use it to make a tone that we can communicate with, but it's not like a muscle that heals – that's why people lose their voice. If you aren't practicing and building back stamina, especially after something as traumatic as heart surgery, it was like an athlete breaking his leg and jumping right back in the game. I think the vocal is a massive instrument. Some people seem to think it's the track versus the vocals. To me the vocal is another instrument in the scheme of the whole track-probably *the most important* of the instruments. Smo's tone is very unique, and because he uses it so much, he needed that recovery time. He took that head-on, and once he found his tone again, we couldn't get him out of the booth!

I can't lie to you. The comeback was not as fierce as I had hoped. It was a struggle to do what used to be so easy. Yes, I had a new heart and felt great, but my body was still getting over the trauma it had endured. I ran on the elliptical every day rapping my whole set over and over trying to get my body ready to go back on the road.

We the People was one of my favorite albums to work on. I had a new production team that saw my vision. I've always loved pushing the limits and thankfully Warner let me have that creative space.

With months of sobriety under my belt, I was writing differently than before. I took an interest in politics during the presidential election that year and decided to really embrace my patriotism. The title track for the album was inspired by Kanye's *Black Skinhead* and the political environment of our country at the time. I also love that song so much because

I wrote it with one of my favorite songwriters Casey Beathard. I even convinced him to keep his original demoed vocal on the final mix. He killed it!

> **Jason:** *We the People* actually came mid record. We were at Dan's house when Smo told me he wanted to use *Hail to the Chief*. The first thing I did was check to see if it was public domain, which thankfully it was, and said, "Alright, I'll see what I can come up with." It started just from taking that sample.

> **Dan:** Musically, Smo had a very specific vision for that song. When we did the song's intro, I ran across the street to borrow a bull horn to record!

We the People is the first album in my career that I ever did sober. I wanted to try to push myself to write about something other than partying. I even have several love songs on the album including the pop track *Never Get Old* with the amazing female vocalist Josie Dunn. I was really excited to get William Michael Morgan as a feature on a song that was very special to me personally, *Thing For You*. That song even has a full stringed quintet playing live on it! It's a beautiful true story.

One of my favorite songs on the *We the People* album is *Say My Name*. It was the first full hip hop track I had done in a really long time and it is one of my favorite songs to this day. Oddly enough, it was number one on the, ahem, "exotic dancing charts". It does have a nice beat if I say so myself. *Movin' on Up* was a real challenge because it was the fastest rapping I had done on a track up to that point. I love it because it has an upbeat happy message with a powerful sing-along chorus.

I'm thankful I had the chance to work with so many talented writers and artists on *We the People*. I'm also thankful to everyone at Warner and to my manager Dan for standing by me during my recovery. We went through a lot together and I'm thankful I had the support.

> **Jason:** I'm not sure I'll ever get to make another album like *We the People*. I couldn't believe Warner just went for it and was like, "Really? Cool!" Smo's musical ability was something that was wonderful to have. I wasn't limited and we didn't have to stay safe. Honestly, that whole record was kind of like, "Just do what you feel like!" Obviously, it has to have some pop to it, but I lean toward pop because I was raised on radio. I think one of the new things we were pushing Smo to do was some of these big pop hooks; *We the People* and *Movin' On Up* were such different tracks than he was used to. They weren't total pop tracks but more like our own country hybrid. I had a great time doing that entire album.

Musically, *We the People* is the most advanced production album I've done to date. It's also the most diverse album I have made and has probably had the most "controversy" so to speak. Because of it, I started the "Don't Genrelize Me" slogan. I felt marginalized by the industry because I wouldn't "pick a genre". What does that even mean? Music is music. I was so tired of people saying my music was too much of one thing or not enough of the other. I experimented with a lot of styles and had a lot of diverse inspiration at the time. *We the People* is one of my favorite albums because I wrote it during such a critical time both personally and professionally. Recovering from heart surgery while recording an album sober had been hard, but I felt so happy and alive. I celebrated finishing the album with a scuba dive adventure with my BFF in Belize.

We The People photo shoot

About midway through the *We the People* tour, my business manager and accountant gave me some troublesome news. We were crunching the numbers for the tour and trying to determine how to come out without a loss. I was regaining momentum from the surgery and trying to get caught up from that setback, but touring was proving to be more and more expensive. If you're not familiar with the music industry, touring has so many expenses. Even if gigs paid really well, I had to pay so many people that Big Smo Inc. wasn't making any profit. They told me that if I kept touring at the rate I was going, I would be bankrupt in three months. I had been with my band for years. We were a close-knit family that had traveled cross country and been on TV together. Sadly, I had to let my band go. We couldn't travel in the tour bus from the show (yes, the one I had *just* bought) because it wasn't reliable, and it was so expensive to fuel and maintain. I would also have to pay a driver and good drivers are hard to find. I had to say goodbye to Mike Lowrey. Thankfully, he continues to be a good buddy of mine.

When I let the band go, I encouraged them to go on an pursue their own careers in music. I am so thankful to have had such a talented group with me. It makes me happen to see them still out in the industry doing what they love. I have nothing but mad love for my band and I will never forget all the years we had together. Venues didn't like much that I didn't have the same "quality of performance" they expected to receive without the band, but doing a track show is what I had to do to keep my business going. I've been thankful enough to have found Keith, my tour manager and part time drummer for back up. I'm also thankful to the venues and fans that still love to see me perform and understand that business is business. Whether it's a live band or some tracks backing me, you're guaranteed to still get one hell of a Smo show!

Conclusion:
FREEDOM

With my hand over my heart
Eyes to the sky
I pledge my allegiance to the stars and the stripes
That's what I was taught
Before I even knew why
The American Dream
Is that why we fight
~ **My Kind America**

As an artist, I've always struggled with wanting to create what I felt in my heart and soul and how to share it with the world. As a human, I've always just wanted to show everyone on the outside who I am on the inside. I don't know where this love for music and passion for words came from. It was something that once I started, it gave me joy or helped me cope, so I kept doing it. Then I met other people that liked music, so we made it together. I never imagined I would have the titles "artist, actor, producer, *rapper*." I didn't set out to be on TV or viral on YouTube, I was just using the platforms popular at the time to share my *music*, my *art*.

Being "famous" is such a weird word to me because it's just a by-prod-uct of what has happened from being successful at what I set out to do. I never imagined people would actually like what I do, what I create, or even like *me*. I think we all as humans struggle with acceptance and believe me, a chubby white kid with skin problems and his own unique fashion sense in the Bible belt of the south during the 1990s was once my reality. Sometimes I laugh when people are in shock or amazement to meet me because in my head, I'm just the excited kid at Camp Box-well or a seventeen-year-old boy trying so hard to find himself. I didn't know what I planned to accomplish when I set out to write this book, but so often I'm asked, "How on earth did you wind up here?" Funny thing, I'm doing the same thing in the same place I've been doing it for the past two decades, and it just so happened the timing was right for the opportunity, and it worked. I was "famous".

Through the journey of writing this book, I've found a new freedom to be myself. My children are older so there are themes that we were are able to be more candid about. I believe the older they get, there are things that are important they know about my own life. I don't want my daughters to ever think I expect them to have it figured out because they are all three surpassing any expectation I could have imagined. I am so proud of all three of them and love them very much. I'm thankful they have stood by me because I know I wasn't always the father I could have been. I hope they can be proud of who I've become in spite of some of my flaws and I hope they know I'm so proud to be their dad.

My only regret is that my dad couldn't be interviewed through this pro-cess. He was my best friend. Even now when I have to make big deci-sions or want to bitch about the flat tire on the mower, I wish I could call my dad. Don't get me wrong, I LOVE my mom, but I just put her through hell the whole first thirty-something years of my life. My dad was always my go-to and I feel like I have a best friend that a lot of you never got to meet. I wish he could have been around, but I know that his influence is still so strong because I notice his voice in my head a lot when I'm doing stuff (stupid shit especially). "John boy, don't do that." That's my favorite. I'm thankful for all the time we had together, and I hope one day I'll be half the man he was.

I want you all to know that the relationship you saw with my mom on the show is real and grew right there live on camera. People in the immediate family were even shocked because my mom and I hadn't really been "friends" before the show. I was just always a pain in her ass. I'm so thankful to her though because she has never given up on me and she is my biggest fan. She knows every show and every appearance and basically every project deadline I have going on, all while still trying to go out and take care of the whole world. She's truly a remarkable mother, grandmother, great-grandmother, sister, aunt, cousin, church lady, domino partner, best friend, she does it all! I'm so thankful to call her my mom. I'm also thankful that she was willing to step up to bat and play ball so to speak because she really was a lot of the heart and joy of the TV show. She has saved my butt way too many times and I'm so blessed we have had such a wild journey together.

It's been kind of tough for our family to talk about the ones that we have lost and the hard times we have had, but it has also been an amazing experience to get to know so much about where I came from.

It's also been very therapeutic to work through some old experiences. I can't take back the bad choices I made, and I didn't write this to brag or seek approval. I want people to know who I am and how I got here. I didn't always do the right thing and I'm sorry to those that I have hurt along the way. We aren't born with the blueprint and so many decisions are made based on circumstance and thinking it's the best or only option. Looking back I don't regret my choices because I'm here today because of every choice I've made. At this point in my life, fame and fortune don't appeal to me. I'm way more focused on my health and happiness these days. Competition doesn't matter anymore and there is plenty of room in this world for legends to coexist and even collaborate.

I have so many ideas for all the music I haven't gotten to make yet, and creatively, I'm still *Workin'*. Luckily, I've been in the industry long enough that I've been able to form new relationships. Those relationships have given me the opportunity to meet and work with some of the most amazing people. I'm living a life beyond my wildest imagination and I'm so thankful to be in the position that financially and contractually, I can make whatever kind of art I want. I'm no longer limited to just music either! Hell, you're holding my *book*. Can you believe it, Neil Gordon? (He's my old art teacher.) Even before the TV show, I loved anything film related. Whether it was in front of or behind the camera, or editing and creating the score, I love creating art on film. The TV show was such as small portion of what I have done when it comes to film, it just got the most attention.

I look forward to doing more film work and have even started a couple of screen plays. It's fun to be this age and in a position to think outside the box. I've also been in the position to work with more and more artists because I'm not bound to any agreement of who I can and can't work with. It's liberating that I'm able to make my dreams happen without so much pressure from the industry. Don't get me wrong, I'm thankful for everything that happened and every experience along the way, but management and labels and network executives are all *real* and they are all *really stressful* to please. I finally feel free to be Smo.

As for financial freedom, I keep working my way toward managing my business in the way that works best to accomplish my goals and take care of my family. I'm thankful to my business partners, Dwight and Katie for their perseverance and patience. I cannot express my gratitude enough for all the financial guidance (and life advice) through every decision I've made both personally and professionally. Thank you for your trust and allowing me to make some risky calls. You've believed in me as an artist and businessman and Big Smo Inc. and I are eternally grateful.

2015 was almost five years ago. I have two graduated daughters that are out making their own way in the world, and Lanica is about to be a junior in high school. Mom is still kicking, and we are thankful she continues to have good health. The farm is pretty quiet these days. I have a cat, a dog, a close-knit group of people I call my family, and a church bus – turned-tiny home to travel around with my best friend. Last year I released *Special Reserve* and I've been on tour with my road manager and drummer Keith this past year.

I've also been working on this book and a new album set to release in the fall called *This One's for You*. If you've kept up with me through socials, you've probably noticed a lot of new collaborations and features. I've met some great people in the California and Colorado Cannabis scenes, and I continue to advocate for the health benefits of cannabis and now live by a "California sober" approach. My newer projects reflect more of my involvement in that community and I'm excited to see what we as Americans have in store for legalization.

I maintain a healthy active lifestyle and am very proud of how far I've come through my health journey. I'm not even *Big* Smo anymore.

As far as my music business, just this week it announced that I signed with Average Joes Entertainment and I'm excited for a new chapter in my life and what opportunities that may hold. I'm thankful to Shannon and everyone on the team at Average Joes.

I've been lucky enough to have David Ray, my new producer and good friend, by my side this year. Thank you for all you've done and I'm excited for the great music we have coming out.

As for the new album, look forward to some surprise appearances and be sure to check out the title track *This One's for You*. Kinfoke, thank you for all the years of love and support. I wouldn't be here without you.

I've been up
I've been down
I was lost
But now I'm found
I had to pick myself up off the ground
Can't stop while the world keeps spinnin' round
I've been broke
I've been bruised
I've had everything to lose
If you're like me, and done kicked the blues,
This one here's for you.

And Now, a Word From My Kinfoke

Glenn Horton, Estill Springs, TN: Hello! I started listening to Big Smo around the summer of 2010. It was inspiring to know that a guy that lived about an hour from me could make it big. I first met Smo at the Estill Springs community center. He brought all the surrounding towns together like true kinfolk doing a benefit for tornado victims from the storms middle Tennessee had just had. He put on one of the best shows and signed every autograph anyone ask of him. Glenn Horton

Tomiese Mason, Connecticut: How do I put in three to five hundred words the effect you had on my father in law in his last months of life? Ugh...Here I go... My wife, sister and brother and law and I were in the back-parking lot preparing, doing what we do waiting for Big Smo, to make his big debut to Laconia. We came from Connecticut to see you because our father is one of your biggest Kinfolk. He would sit and watch all your videos, knew all the words to your songs...and would always say how we wished he could just go down to Tennessee and just be in your presence. He related to you on so many levels just off your music. He didn't just listen to your music. He felt every word. We had these tickets for your show for months! We saw this bus pull in the parking lot. Laughing, I'm like "Wouldn't that be funny if that was his tour bus?" Long behold...you wouldn't be you if you didn't ride the way you ride! (RESPECT IT!)

I quickly call our Dad who's in the front already waiting in line to get into the Whiskey Barrel's doors to see you and I say to him "Get back here right now...Here's here! His bus is here. They're unloading equipment. I SEE HIM!" Before I can even finish that sentence my dad was already next to me. It's like he flew, so we walked to the back of your tour bus and he came up to you and he said, "I just want to shake your hand. It's such an honor to shake your hand," and I told you when he walked away our daddy didn't have much longer to live. He was battling cancer and seeing you was on his bucket list. He just adored you. Then,

YOU called him on that stage, and you made him dream come true. You made him finally become the ROCK STAR that he always believed he was. You guys did Kickin it in Tennessee together and my family and I never in my life seen the joy and happiness you gave him. You have no idea what you did for him Smo. You are an amazing person for that. Just know that you have an Angel Kinfoke. And our Dad is Kickin in Heaven still listening to your music and being a Rockstar!

Adam and Bailey. Tallahassee FL: Hey, I'm Adam and I started jamming to your tunes in 2016 when I was a heavy haul driver in the military. Your album Bringing it Home stood out on the shelf at Walmart and I figured well I gotta try it out. Well I got hooked to say the least. Weather I was in the truck or on the trails of Alaska your songs always matched and made me feel close to home. After I separated from service and went home to Panama City Florida, my wife and I were waiting till you had a tour stop close enough for us to go to. Well our prayers were finally answered when you stopped in Destin unscheduled in October of 2017. My wife and I had a blast and I was so happy to finally meet

Sleeping on Tour bus

Backstage in the greenroom

Rocking Out on the Harp

Hangin with Kuntry

A sold-out show live

Me and the crew

At The Machine Shop in Flint MI

Come See For Yourself

Backstage with The LACs

Chief Keith my Tour Manger & Drummer

The band will aways be my family

Dan Sigmund my BEST Merch guy

Kuntry's Son - X - My Lil Homie

Me & all 3 of my daughters

Ameria, My First College Graduate

Mama Smo and me at Ameria's
High School graduation

Lanica's 15th Birthday

The Women In My World

Ameria's Graduation Celebration at church

Kisses from Lanica

Ansley on Prom Night

Growin' Up Fast

Love my Pearl Squirrel

Love my Mama

Me and Family at Christmas

Cooking with the
Fire Department

My Wild Man Moment

Reppin' that Down Yonder Apparel

Me, Steve, and Ladybug

Me and Jake on Jan 28, 2017 COUNTRY RAP Documentary shoot at farm

The Moonshine Bandits out at the farm

Love me Some DOWN YONDER Apparel

Hosier, Upchurch & Me

Me and Demun Jones

Show Time With Shotgun Shane

Me & Irlene Mandrell

RIP Mac Miller

Tennessee Stix and me

My Country Outlaw video

Afroman & Me

Shooting with RATED RED

I shot that cannon and hit a tree

The Mufreesboro WORKIN' video shoot

My Good Friend Blue Smoke BBQ

And the Local Fireman Award
goes to Me

CMA FEST 2017

Hangin with the BIG DOGS

190

Hog Huntin' with the Florida Crew &
J.T. Money

Bone Splitta

Beto reppin' that swag

Me and the popo

In the Studio with the Bandits

One of my Best Friends Rodney Yoes

Me with Joelie & Mikaiah at CMA Fest

The Plug - My Good Friend Logan

Detroit Muscle TV Show

You gotta be a Hustler to get it like me

Working on the weed farm in Chico, CA

you in person. You provided a down home feel not a lot of artist offer. Well in October this past year as you know Hurricane Michael came through and destroyed everything luckily my wife and I were able to salvage most of our belongings including the poster and flag you signed a year prior and it was in the most damaged part of our home we were extremely happy those pulled through. The lyrics "when going gets tough the tough pull through it" rang in my head as my wife are now finally getting back to level ground. Kinfolk for life.

Christy "G" Stalder and Missy Raitch, Ohio: At the Garage Bar in Barberton, Ohio. Smo put on awesome show as always. But my story starts, after the show... We hung out at a "Motorcycle Groups" club house. The stories were-a-flowin' and the smoke was-a-risin'. In the midst of all this, a baby skunk comes strolling by. Smo said "Stay still there's a skunk." My friend, Missy, squeals and runs (city girl). Luckily, lil Pepe Le Pew just kept it movin' odor free. While talking with Smo, he just ask where we were staying that night, because he knew we were couple hours from home. Well needless to say, my DD (Missy) was hammered and I wasn't far behind. No reservations had been made and its 3 a.m., so I told him we were gonna sleep in my car. Being one of the nicest people you'll ever meet, Smo said he was rolling out to next show, after he showered at his hotel. So this teddy bear of a man gave us his hotel room. That's the night we went from Kinfoke4life to Friends4life!!!

Tami Purcell, Guns, Pinball and Porsches: It was a memorable day on our 30-acre ranch. Why? Smo dropped in! You all know how he loves being outside. We invited him and Cruz to come visit our ranch and use it to shoot some promotional pictures. While there we thought he might like to try out the shooting range if he had time before his big show at the Cotton Eyed Joe that same evening. He arrived in the early afternoon and we had a ball riding the 4-wheeler on our trails with the sun set low in the distance. It wasn't long before Smo noticed he was missing some clothes he needed for his planned photo session. My husband popped around the corner dressed in barn clothes and a .38 strapped to his hip.

I asked him if he could give Smo a ride back to the Cotton Eyed Joe to pick up the clothing. He couldn't get the smile off his face – he asked Smo to jump in the passenger seat of his Porsche 911 Carrera S and they tore off down the quarter mile long driveway toward the Joe. Smo said they hit over 135MPH on the way and they got back in what seemed like seconds! The rest of that day was just beautiful – a sunny and unusually warm day in November.

When Cruz and he were done with the photo shoot we spent more than an hour on our private shooting range where Cruz proceeded to surprise us all by being an amazing first-time shooter. Smo got to shoot my husbands .500 S&W magnum (like pulling the trigger on three .44 magnum shells all at the same time!). Smo went live on Facebook to share the event. We shot until is started to get dark and then moved the party in to the ranch house. It was time to play some PINBALL! We have a collection of over 30 machines and Smo loves to play. We set up the new AC/DC for a 4-player game and went to town. We all love music and it's hard not to get your toes tappin' and hips moving to a little hard rock. Though the game was new to him Smo played like a pro and had a steady smile on his face. I love watching others enjoy the collection and having Smo there made it extra special.

Before show time, he likes to eat something lite and healthy. I'm gluten free and super careful about my diet and Smo knows and trusts that I'll make him something special and healthy. I set about making a green salad, added some fruit and nuts along with my famous homemade balsamic vinegar/ olive oil/rosemary dressing. He took his time eating to savor every bite. But now, it was time – the show must go on. We jumped in my Macan S (with Smo at the wheel I might add) cranked up some fresh Smo tunes and headed to the Joe to start the show. That day I learned that Kinfoke doesn't have to be about relatives. Smo is like a brother, he is family and always will be.

Kristen Wagoner, Conway, Arkansas: My favorite story is when they gave me a microphone to sing with them, what a fun night.

Tee Robinson, Chattanooga, TN: Alan and I first met you in 2015 at Lake Winnie we were there for Alan's birthday and his daughter was in the hospital with complications with her pregnancy. We had talked about that when we stopped to chat with you in the park. A few months later we came to see you again in Clarksville. We got there early and was parked outside by your bus. You came out to let everyone outside know that you wouldn't be staying after the show because you had to fly out right after the show. You approached us and immediately remembered us from lake Winnie and remembered that Alan's daughter had been in the hospital with pregnancy complications and you asked how that went Alan dropped his head and you just knew she had lost the baby. You told him say no more you went to your bus and got a picture and autographed it to Shelby Alan's daughter. Even after months of not see-ing you at a show and seeing so many people you remembered and never forgot. A few years later Alan got a Kinfoke tattoo with the date of his granddaughter's death tatted underneath which was Alan's birthday we came to see you in Murfreesboro and showed you the tat he had gotten 1 was because of the mad respect we had for you and 2 in honor of his granddaughter. You still remembered a few years later and never forgot.

You are truly an amazing human being with such a great soul. You never forget where you came from and always show compassion and kindness to everyone you meet. We'll always have mad respect and love for you. You're like family to us now and always will be. #Kinfoke4Life

Will Madison, Toccoa, GA: Never have I met an artist such as you, Big Smo. You're a very genuine guy with an obvious love for your fans. In 2010, I went through a period in my life where I suffered from extreme depression. I first discovered you and your music the same year. I listened to your music and it helped pull me through that rough time in my life. I have been a fan ever since. Your music helped me discover who I really wanted to be; I still am that person to this day. Thank you, The Mad General

Robert & Amanda Ratliff, Lakeland/Fort Meyers, Florida – Greenville, Tennessee: We got to go to 3 different concerts of yours and we enjoyed the whole concert. You throw a heck of a show. We done a meet and greet at all 3 concerts. Have auto graphs, towels, pictures with my kids. It is truly amazing what you do for the kids. Keep it up cause my kids love your music as do we!!! Julie Kay, Spanaway, Washington: Raye smudged you (Native American blessing), you got squeaked in as Gerbil in the man cave and massaged by Natalie (the Air Force flight medic) ... I hope you had a great time. We sure did. You ever need anything holla I got you family baby-bruddah rideordie. You're a good egg Smo keep on, keeping it real!!

Michelle Hickson, Tennessee: So I guess I knew you before I knew of you. Take us back to the Child Development Center and hours of sitting through therapy for our precious little ones. Then I met you, and Diddle and I always enjoyed time spent with you and your girls at the house swimming or just hanging for a good time. We got to partake in one of your first videos with THE JEEP and it was a great time, and let's not forget turkey burgers in your back yard. You were at times too much for me but never too much for Diddle, and thus we loved you. Those years ago, you dearly treasured close friends and friendships, I hope that is still true. You were a great dad to your girls, and a great friend. And watching your success has been a real joy. Best wishes to you always in all that you do, from your old school friends Michelle and Diddle.

Michael Gentry Athens, GA: Probably not the coolest story but a buddy of mine and I went to the Athens, Ga show. While standing in line Smo walks out on the sidewalk to listen to the street preacher. Smo and I had a pretty good conversation while getting called all sorts of sinners by the nut job across the street. The show was awesome! I have seen many shows at the Georgia Theater, and this was the first time I know of that a band or entertainer came out on the street to hang out. This is a testament of how in touch Smo is with his fans. See the YouTube link below, I am the guy in the brown jacket. 2/12/2916 https://youtu.be/ Ro57rPQKtaI

Tee Robinson, Tennessee: One word… BRISTOL!

Dannielle McCullough, Bucyrus, Ohio: I met Smo at Dillinger's in Bucyrus. The first time I saw his show there and got his autograph, then I talked to him about coming and making a surprise visit at the Jericho House Recovery House for Women. That's when I got to see the Real side of Smo, not the stage personality but John Smith. The down-to-earth person who faces hard times and who faces life like the rest of us, and that's when I knew I'd be a fan for life. I got my picture taken with him, and also got an autograph that time but it was more of a personal one I played Smo while pregnant with my tiny human, and then sent him a video of it. That autograph is framed it means the world to me. KINFOLK 4LIFE…

Michael Donati, Port Saint Lucie FL: Just a shout out to Big Smo. I was out at 74 Family Fun Park getting my adrenaline rush on at the Dirt Drag Strip. While I was at my trailer in the pits, I met these two guys from Florida Wildlife Adventure, it just so happens we were talking about you and the one guy was talking to you on video chat to you and let me talk to you live on his phone. I thought that was very cool made my night, hope to catch you in person out there soon!

Debra Vickers, Dayton, KY: It started out on a nice Oct, day I had just lost 2 of my brothers 12 days apart. I had stopped on Monmouth St. in Newport, KY collecting donations for a fund raiser for my brothers. I was standing there talking to a friend of mind that just so happens to be the mayor of Newport, KY. He looks up and sees your bus coming down Monmouth St. and he said, "Big Smo." I said, "BIG SMO?" with such a surprise, I said, "Jerry, I got to go it is Big Smo, I got to go see Big Smo!" I ran home to pick my grandsons up from school and I told them where are going to go see Big Smo they were so excited they had known you from Lizard Lick the song you sang about the lick. So we get there and we go thru the back door, and you was hooking up wires for the sound system, I came in and tapped you on the shoulder and said "What up kinfolk," and you were so nice and took a pic with me and my grandsons and were then nice enough to take the time to take a pic with each one of us. We were so happy that we got to meet you. The boys went to school the next day and was bragging about getting their pic with Big Smo, and myself I was so happy also I bought some of your barbecue sauce, then came to your show that night and it was a badass performance. I would love to see you come back and do another show, so I just wanted to say you are such an awesome person to drop what you was doing to take a pic with us and Thank you very much. So keep it up because you are the best Country Rapper there is, Rock on and Thank you again so much!

Danny Yager, Louisville, KY: The Man, The Myth and Straight of the Kuntry. Big Smo is one of the most down to earth Singers I have ever met. A few years back he came to Louisville. It was one of the best concerts I've ever seen. I appreciate it Smo taking your time out to meet the fans. Keep Working!

Justin Johnson, Charlotte, NC: Been hooked since you did song "*Hick Life.*" I ordered a CD back in the day, never received it, so I called you and you didn't hesitate to send me what I ordered. Now fast forward, I still kept in contact and I live in Charlotte, 20 min from the Long Branch in Rock Hill, S.C., and I brought you some homemade wine to you on your bus, but you were sick. Have been to a couple of your shows since then u still the man and I'm still a super fan keep doin your thing.

Betty Codispoti, Tennessee: I had recently moved to Tennessee and the only singer I hoped to meet was Smo. I was working in a local grocery store and along comes a guy I recognize so I whisper to myself, "He looks like my Smo!" and he leans over and says, "Because he is Smo!" I apologized first and then asked for a hug, I now scan the store constantly watching to "get lucky" again.

Tammy Stamper, Quincey, Kentucky: Hey Smo, My name is Tammy and I met you in Florida at The Roundup. I have pics with you and we actually spoke on the phone. I think you are an awesome person and I had a blast that night! I live in Quincy Kentucky and I'm a small-town girl that loves your music. Hope all is well and keep on keeping on! Gary Turnbo: You were in a cow pasture at Big John birthday party. I think we were the oldest people at the party, the cops show up and we ran till they left. Great party!!!

Joannie Lynch, Texas: How about that time you and Gary Lynch from Tx-4 Texas kinfoke partied so hard you both had so much red stag the bar cut y'all off and wouldn't let y'all have any more alcohol man you all were toasted that was Gary's favorite. Mine would he the night in Nacogdoches Texas when I accidentally knocked off the meat mud and it busted everywhere, and you stopped the whole show and asked what pissed me off... ha ha ha

Tee Layton, Lakeland, FL: Smo booked an event in Lakeland again so I bought tickets. It was the 3rd time I got to see him in concert. The day of the concert a really good friend of mine passed away and I almost didn't go but decided to go anyway and very happy I did. I told him about my friend, and he said he was glad I came, and did I enjoy the show. He is such an awesome down to earth person that kicks it with his Kinfoke, and he keeps it real. Been a fan since TV love ya Smo and always will be KF4L.

Toni Ford, Tennessee: I've been coming to a lot of your concerts and shows and parties of so much fun' Hands Down to You 'the best of the best!! Wow couldn't get any better kicking it with you is the best days of my life as I travel to see you in so many places I wouldn't have it any other way ' from VIP to out in the crowd to you jumping off stage to get beside me and us laugh and having fun. #Kinfoke 4life, Much love.

Sarah Kimbler, Richmond, KY: So a couple years back, you had come to Richmond. I wanted to go so bad not only because I was a fan, but it was my birthday. A friend of mine tried to call numerous times to have me come meet you but my phone died. So they next morning I got all my voicemails. I was balling my eyes out the guy who tried calling me was walking across the street. I guess he had told you everything that was going on and you gave him a signed CD and t-shirt for me which I still have and cherish very much. Thank you for the CD and shirt.

Lisa Aguilera, California: Hey Big Smo... this should be fun reading all these stories! So here is mine! My ex-boyfriend is a huge fan of yours and for his birthday back in 2016, I surprised him with a trip to Sacramento to see you perform at Ace of Spades. We got up there early and as we were walking to dinner, we ran into you and another guy. I told you he was a big fan and you offered for us to hang out. Anyway, the good thing that came out of that relationship is that he introduced me to your music!

Victoria Jordan, Borden, IN: The year was 2015, the venue was The Mercury Ballroom Louisville, KY. My brother Delmas (Chris) Couch was one of your biggest fans. Y'all kinda even looked alike. He lived the life of your songs, especially *Kickin' It In Tennessee.* Well he was SO excited to see you he bought the WHOLE VIP section and was gonna take all his friends to see you. But I guess that just wasn't in the cards because you had to cancel the April show because I do believe of your Heart Surgery. You rescheduled for August and my brother died 4-8-15 of a massive heart attack. So me and my family came to the show, and in the merch line I told you it really reminded me a lot of Dragon Heart and that you were the young prince with a piece of the dragon's heart now. You took a step back and said I really blew your mind. I still believe this and think it would make a great song. Hope to see you in IN! Forever your Fan.

Janene Collins, Dayton Ohio: I had the privilege of meeting you for the first time at Oddbody's in the Dayton Ohio in November 2018. I was so excited that you stuck around after the show to talk with your fans. You are just amazing and put on one hell of a show!!! This was the second time seeing you in concert. You never disappoint!!! I can't wait until you come back again!!! Keep doing what you're doing!!! Love you Big Smo!!!!

Joe Stixxx, Georgia: I was a fan and was really looking forward to seeing his show and I told him how we drove all the way from Ga to Nashville and we wanted to kick it with him. So he invited us to his house, and we kicked it in the studio and got to listen to all the shit he was working on for the kinfoke album. It was dope AF. He actually recorded a song with us and put it on that album it was a song called White Boy and it was awesome. When we left there me and sine stixxx formed a group called The Stixxx and the rest was history. Thanks for the kick ass time Big Smo.

Chad Brewer, Springfield, MO: Hey Smo, So it's my girl's birthday. 1st one since we are together. I was an Army soldier married 20 years and divorced when I came back from Afghanistan in 2011. This new girl, Jessica, is awesome. Liked the Bandits. Liked Smo. Now I married her. I took her to Springfield, MO for her Birthday. I set up the tickets to see Smo. Didn't know The Lacs would be there or anyone else. We show up. This is in the Shrine, I am Freemason, so I feel at home. We grab some beers and stand watching the show. I start yelling "Smo." Everyone around me laughs and starts yelling Smo. You come out and fist pump the air. Unfortunately by the time I have received your set list from those around me, and get your autograph, I am tore up. Too much fun at home. LOL. Really appreciate your music. You really makes some of the best music I have ever heard.

MaryAnn Frisby Little Rock, Arkansas: August 2014, Big Smo played at Juanita's in Little Rock Arkansas. Big Smo is always gracious to his fans. We ate at the restaurant there before the show, he was at the bar and accommodated us with a pic.

Pat Baldwin, Spokane, Washington: My Wife and I were waiting in line to meet you, and my wife spilled a beer on the Bouncer she was all upset, and you told her it was all good #AwesomeConcert #goodtimes

A Few Words From the Homies

I would absolutely say he's been a pioneer."
Bird Brooks, The Moonshine Bandits

"I think what I admired most about Smo was the
business sense that he had, and sense to get the reality
TV show and get the big deal. I just remember thinking
'That will do a lot for this genre and put this genre
on the map where it needs to be.' "
Clay Sharpe, The LACs

"I think he's one of the first people who gave a lot
of these country boys a voice and made them feel
like it was cool to be from the sticks."
Demun Jones

"Smo's a genius. When the National Enquirer called
Smo a 'Country Singer,' I almost had a stroke!"
HAYSTAK

Jake Brown
Dedication & Thanks

I'd like to dedicate this book to my dogs, our late, great cocker spaniel Little Hannie and our adorable Westie Molly Wobs. Both of these dogs sat at my feet MANY a late night for months on end over the past 2 ½ years working on this book, and I sure appreciate the company and comradery.

First, thank you to SMO for the opportunity to make this my 50th published book in 20 years and definitely one of my top 2 or 3 favorites, definitely one of my proudest book projects to ever hit store shelves, I had a blast writing with you the past 3 years, thanks again for the hon-or! Thank you Darlene Swanson for the fantastic job with the layout!; thank You to the entire team at our amazing publisher, BAKER & TAYLOR – especially Geoff Emerick, Tim Leonhart, Jason Seidel, and Mark Hillesheim; the wonderful women at our pressing partner, McNaughton-Gunn – especially Brenda Coo, et all for the quick turnaround on books; Thank you to my wife Carrie for putting up with my schedule; Thank you to my in-laws Bill and Susan, Thanks to my always-supportive parents James and Christina Brown, my brother Ret. Sgt. Joshua T. Brown, US Army, and the extended Brown, Thieme and Brock families; my gang (Alex, Cris, Drew, Sean, Bob, Paul & Helen, Richard Kendrick, and anyone else whose still with me after all these years); Aaron Harmon, Ray "Orig Riddle, and anyone else who helped make this book a reality, thanks to you all.

Co-Author Bio

Award-winning Music biographer Jake Brown has written 50 published books over the past 20 years, featuring many authorized collaborations with some of rock's biggest artists, including 2013 Rock & Roll Hall of Fame inductees Heart (with Ann and Nancy Wilson), living guitar legend Joe Satriani, blues legend Willie Dixon (authorized w/the Estate), country music legends Merle Haggard/Freddy Powers, heavy metal pioneers Motorhead (with Lemmy Kilmister), country rap superstar Big Smo, late hip hop icon Tupac Shakur (with the estate), and many more. Brown is also author of a variety of anthology series including 'Nashville Songwriter' Vol I and II; 'Behind the Boards' Vol. 1 and 2; 'Beyond the Beats' Vol. I and II" and the 'Hip Hop Hits' producers' series among many others. Brown recorded audio books for Blackstone Audio, including such titles as "Doctors of Rhythm," "Beyond the Beats," "Scientists of Sound" and "Prince in the Studio," and recently saw his "Beyond the Beats" and Prince books published in Japan. Brown has also appeared as the featured biographer of record on Fuse TV's Live Through This series, Bloomberg TV's Game Changers series, and in all 6-parts of the BET "The Death Row Chronicles" docuseries. In 2012, Brown won the Association for Recorded Sound Collections Awards in the category of Excellence in Historical Recorded Sound Research.